On Broken Legs

On Broken Legs

A SHATTERED LIFE, A SEARCH FOR GOD, A MIRACLE

THAT MET ME IN A CAVE IN ASSISI

WENDY MURRAY ZOBA

NAVPRESS®

BRINGING TRUTH TO LIFE

OUR GUARANTEE TO YOU

We believe so strongly in the message of our books that we are making this quality guarantee to you. If for any reason you are disappointed with the content of this book, return the title page to us with your name and address and we will refund to you the list price of the book. To help us serve you better, please briefly describe why you were disappointed. Mail your refund request to: NavPress, P.O. Box 35002, Colorado Springs, CO 80935.

The Navigators is an international Christian organization. Our mission is to reach, disciple, and equip people to know Christ and to make Him known through successive generations. We envision multitudes of diverse people in the United States and every other nation who have a passionate love for Christ, live a lifestyle of sharing Christ's love, and multiply spiritual laborers among those without Christ.

NavPress is the publishing ministry of The Navigators. NavPress publications help believers learn biblical truth and apply what they learn to their lives and ministries. Our mission is to stimulate spiritual formation among our readers.

Published in association with Eames Literary Services, Nashville, Tennessee.

NAVPRESS, BRINGING TRUTH TO LIFE, and the NAVPRESS logo are registered trademarks of NavPress. Absence of ® in connection with marks of NavPress or other parties does not indicate an absence of registration of those marks.

ISBN 1-57683-643-6

Cover design by David Carlson Design
Cover image: Johner/Photonica
Creative Team: Rachelle Gardner, Arvid Wallen, Darla Hightower, Glynese Northam

Some of the anecdotal illustrations in this book are true to life and are included with the permission of the persons involved. All other illustrations are composites of real situations, and any resemblance to people living or dead is coincidental.

Unless otherwise identified, all Scripture quotations in this publication are taken from the *Holy Bible, New Living Translation* (NLT), copyright © 1996. Used by permission of Tyndale House Publishers, Inc., Wheaton, Illinois 60189. All rights reserved. Other versions used include: the *New King James Version* (NKJV). Copyright © 1982 by Thomas Nelson, Inc. Used by permission. All rights reserved; and the *King James Version* (KJV).

Zoba, Wendy Murray.
  On broken legs : a shattered life, a search for God, a miracle that met me in a cave in Assisi / by Wendy Murray Zoba.-- 1st ed.
     p. cm.
  Includes bibliographical references.
  ISBN 1-57683-643-6
  1. Zoba, Wendy Murray. 2. Christian biography--United States. I. Title.
  BR1725.Z63A3 2004
  2773'082'092--dc22   2004012717

Printed in Canada
1 2 3 4 5 6 7 8 9 10 / 08 07 06 05 04

FOR A FREE CATALOG OF
NAVPRESS BOOKS & BIBLE STUDIES,
CALL 1-800-366-7788 (USA)
OR 1-416-499-4615 (CANADA)

for Carol, my sis,
my safe place
T

CONTENTS

FOREWORD

⟡

The dying and rising of our Lord Jesus Christ constitute the heart of Christianity, and this death-resurrection pattern is reproduced in different ways in the lives of all believers — all, that is, whose true identity is that they died and are now risen in and with their Savior. The symbolism of their baptism — going under water to signify death, and coming out of the water to signify resurrection — points to this, and it becomes the recurring quality of their life-experience. Death-feelings, followed by the peace and joy of resurrection, form much of the inside story of their discipleship. The "desert" and the "dark night of the soul" are among the descriptions that the first stage of the cycle evokes.

Paul had been there, either through illness or through threats on his life, and says so: "We were so utterly burdened beyond our strength that we despaired of life itself. Indeed, we felt that we had received the sentence of death. But that was to make us rely not on ourselves but on God who raises the dead. He delivered us . . ." (2 Corinthians 1:8-10). "Dying, and behold we live" (6:9) was how Paul described his ongoing existence.

Wendy Zoba also has been there, and gifted writer that she is, she now lifts the veil on her passage through the dry places to help us all to more sober and realistic devotion to our Lord.

Next to me as I write is a brochure for *Outward Bound* courses. "The wilderness," it says, "will be your classroom. The lakes, rivers, forests, mountains, and ocean provide the challenges.... The rewards come from meeting these challenges and accomplishing what you thought was impossible.... You'll be compelled to dig deep...."

The Christian life is God's *Upward Bound* course, and has a similar prospectus with relationships and circumstances in place of the physical geography. It is a course that we are all called to take. On broken feet? Well, yes, very often so. Wendy's story will help us all at this point. Walk with her, and learn more about the ways of God with those whom he loves and is nurturing for glory.

—J. I. PACKER
Regent College

ACKNOWLEDGMENTS

I wish to thank my agent, John Eames, for believing in me, for owning this project, and for bringing it to the attention of Dan Rich at NavPress. I thank Dan for the vision he saw for it and for allowing me the chance to see it through. This could not have been done without the brilliant instincts and remarkable demeanor of my editor, Rachelle Gardner, who walked each step of this narrative with me, strengthening it (and me), reassuring me, and giving me the map I needed to get through it.

I've read occasionally in authors' acknowledgments how the author could not have written the book without this person having done that, or another person having done such and so. Whereas the writing of this book has been for me a lonely project, getting me to the place in my life where I could again put pen to paper has indeed been the fruit of others' vigilance and watch-care over me. They are the unseen players in this narrative. I can't say how many people prayed and otherwise helped me through this passage. They know who they are, and I thank them.

Remember Jesus of Nazareth, staggering on broken feet
out of the tomb toward Resurrection, bearing on his body
the proud insignia of defeat which is victory,
the magnificent defeat of the human soul
at the hands of God.

FREDERICK BUECHNER

ENDINGS

This book tracks the journey of a wife and mother who fell into a hole. She had been the kind of mother who made special cakes and chocolate chip cookies for surprise birthday parties. She'd read her Bible and gone to church and in fact had been married to the believing community's treasured prize, a pastor. I am that wife and mother, and my hope and sense of personhood had resided in these identities.

The hole started as a crack, a fissure that was barely noticeable. In the stories of our lives we all have cracks, don't we? For a long time, the weak spot sustained the weight of the trappings called my life: flowerbeds, young men and their girlfriends, neighbors, church. The church added special weight. Over time, almost imperceptibly, the fissure grew more pronounced.

When I fell into the hole, I lost my marriage to divorce and my three grown sons to the "empty nest." One devastating season threw into chaos everything I'd believed, upheld, written about, and stood upon when it came to understanding who I was in this world.

I sadly remember the day in January 2003 when the space shuttle Columbia disintegrated during reentry. A small lesion had been introduced by, of all things, a piece of foam. The damage was so minor, and foam so seemingly nonabrasive, the blemish seemed irrelevant. We all know now that neither the foam nor the fissure were irrelevant. We know that a single, barely noticeable weak spot can become a point of entry for dangerous effusions that push a mighty machine beyond the laws of physics to cross an invisible line and commence a fiery chain reaction. Once thus overtaken, the Columbia had only one way to go: straight to earth in broken pieces across Texas.

Being a pastor's family, we tried heroically to ignore the crack. So many people do not want pastors' families to have cracks. Pastors' families are the ones other families look to for the picture of "the Christian home." This is not a book about the pressures faced by pastors' families (though there needs to be such a book). It is a book about how, after the weak spot in one pastor's family couldn't sustain the weight of the world it upheld, the crack opened, the chain reaction commenced, and everything fell to broken pieces across the landscape of my life. That's when the mother slid into the hole. Then it closed in over her. She groped in darkness. Until, in God's timing, she found a way out.

I call the hole the Dark Night. It hearkens the term coined by St. John of the Cross when he referred to "the dark night of the soul," a time of spiritual search and demonic oppression so severe that it pushes the outer limits of belief in God and even one's sanity. G. K. Chesterton wrote, "We used to be told in the nursery that if a man were to bore a hole through the centre of the earth and climb continually down and down, there would come a moment at the centre when he would seem to be climbing up and up."[1] This book is about that: falling into the hole; boring (blindly) through its seemingly endless levels; crossing the line where the descent moved to an ascent; the climb out; the near insanity; the death I died; and the life I found when by God's mercy I stepped out on the other side.

The reader will understand that the sad events relating to my divorce are deeply personal and sacred. Christian people, and others I suppose, always wonder in the case of divorce if adultery was involved. Whereas the issues that brought about the collapse of my marriage are not detailed in this book, I will offer what solace I can by assuring the reader no adultery was involved. This is not a book about my failed marriage. It is a book about how I clawed through the wreckage after the devastation. It is about how my faith in God caved in; about how I broke down and lost hope, and for a time abdicated belief that God was present in this dark, sad place. It is about my search for God there, and about how, as I kept scratching, even in shadows, he showed himself.

What's funny is, I came to understand that the journey itself was an answer to the very prayers I'd stopped believing in. People who know me attest that my greatest strength and most profoundly dangerous weakness is my fighting Scot (Murray clan) heart's fire — so-called "passion." It lands me in equal parts on the edges of the sublime and in the center of the ridiculous. During one such flourish as my life collapsed around me, I called to God as with a raised spear: Bring on the dogs of war! Would that I had better communicated *I was kidding*. I've since apologized for the sarcasm.

Once inside the hole, in any case, the heart-fire business went out. The passage went dark, cold, and wet. I questioned everything I'd believed, and I heard no answers to my praying.

The writer of the book of Hebrews wrote: "While Jesus was

here on earth, he offered prayers and pleadings, with a loud cry and tears, to the one who could deliver him out of death. And God heard his prayers because of his reverence for God. So even though Jesus was God's Son, he learned obedience from the things he suffered."[2] Jesus' cries and tears compelled me to explore the possibility that if Jesus, being the Son, had to suffer to be heard, maybe cries and tears were the way in.

But who wants that? Can't we just relate to God by registering needs and complaints and desires and slippages and so on — and leave it at that?

One author I was reading at the time posed the question, "Suppose mountains, victimized by myriads of prayers, gamboled like lambs."[3] Do we want that? What do we really want when we pray? What happens? If mountains don't move, what does? This book tracks the journey that, for me, answered that question.

In Dante's allegory *The Divine Comedy*, he navigates layers of nether hell with a guide, the ancient poet Virgil. For Dante, the journey is alarming and disorienting in the extreme. He confronts, incrementally, a deeper darkness. His guide Virgil explains the route as best he can. For example, he says in the first level they encounter "the heretics"; in the second, those who did "violence against their neighbor"; the third, violence against self; and so on. At one point, feeling he'd journeyed as far as he could, Dante exclaimed:

> "O Master dear, that seven times over again
> Hast brought me safely through," said I, "and freed
> From all the perils that in my path have lain,

Leave me not utterly undone! Indeed,
If we may not go forward, pray let's quit,
And hasten back together with all good speed!"

Alas, the course could not be reversed. Virgil responded:

"Fear no whit;
There's none at all can stay our steps, nor make thee
Forbear the pass: such Power hath granted it.

Wait for me here; to cheerful thoughts betake thee;
Feed thy faint heart with hope, and calm thy breast,
For in this underworld I'll not forsake thee."[4]

Like Dante, I had a Guide who prodded me through my underworld, though many were the times I could not see him. Also like Dante, I found myself hankering to turn back, or in any case, not to go on. My Guide nudged me on, even when I could not perceive his location.

Now I will be your guide as we enter the treacherous landscape called the Dark Night. It is a disorienting place: At moments in the descent you feel an upward lean; at other moments during the ascent, you feel a downward slide. In some places, the course tarries and it seems we'll never move on. At other places, glimpses of light come in such small pieces that we blink and ask ourselves, *Did I just see that?* Hold on. We'll get through. Let your questions abide until we have stepped into the light. The gift of hindsight will clarify the steps.

The stages of my journey are located in seasons of my life that met them, rounding out a bit more than a year. The chapter titles serve as a kind of map that will help orient, if only minimally. For example, the first test I confronted after slipping into the hole was the relinquishment of terms by which my life could be saved; "Surrender the Terms" tracks that leg of the journey. Still getting my bearing, chapter 2, "Bless the Mundane," describes a kind of "pep talk" that arrived from an unexpected place. I would discover it girded me and gave me tools I'd need to face the journey ahead, day in and day out. Then on we went, my invisible Guide and I, into the chaos, described in chapter 3, "Enter the Chaos." And on it goes. Chapter after chapter describes the incremental descent that in time became a tortured ascent, though in the midst of it, these demarcations were not so clearly discernable. That is the gift of hindsight.

I faced a test at each stage. To this day, I do not know how I managed to "pass," if indeed I did pass. I assume I did, if for no other reason than that new tests kept coming and, as my son has said by way of encouragement, "You're not dead yet." In any case, if I passed, it has not been by virtue of my own will or devotion. Desperation, perhaps, like Peter's backhanded confession to Jesus. Jesus had spoken a "hard teaching," and as a result many followers deserted him. He turned to his impetuous disciple and asked if he would be leaving too. Peter said, "To whom would we go?"[5]

Thomas Merton calls such testing the "interrogation of suffering." He says that if we, as God's own offspring, are intended to be alive in the way he created us to be, "the interrogation of suffering will call forth from us both our name and the name of Jesus."[6] I take that to mean that by the end of this process, if it hasn't killed you, it will have made you who you were meant to be. But only by virtue of resurrection after another kind of death, which is where the union with Jesus comes into it, by God's grace.

He promised me as Virgil did Dante, that "in this underworld I'll not forsake thee." Neither will I forsake you as we pass this way together. It is my hope and plea that if you are lost somewhere in the Dark Night, that by God's mercy his hand will reach you through my hand and my story, so that once we are through it, you will know your own name, and the name of Jesus too.

Fall

CHAPTER ONE

SURRENDER THE TERMS

*begin in the fall because that was when my divorce papers were filed, though the feelings exacted from such an event cannot be measured by days or months on a calendar. That September the fissure, as I've described it, gave way to collapse and I slipped into the breach. No adequate words describe what the collapse felt like, nor the subsequent disorientation. Little things that once made up the ballast of my life were carried away as if by rushing waters: chats with neighbors, phone calls from friends, cookouts, and bike rides to the pool. I found support, of a kind, from a few chosen friends during that time. Practical help was something else. I needed to have a garage sale and kept thinking I'd receive offers to help. I couldn't manage a garage sale in the best of times and was hopeless during this crisis. But no offers came. Once when I was still living with my husband, an old friend visited, a pastor, and funnily, I thought he'd be, well, pastoral about what was happening. We'd shared good times before the day he visited, and I thought he'd say, "Why don't we three go out for coffee?" I pictured him wanting to help us both. But when I walked into the room where he was chatting with my husband, the way he said a muted hello signaled he did not mean to rise from his chair. Oddly, I'd already made the awkward motions of greeting him with a hug, and so he was constrained to rise and force his smile. For a strained three minutes I sat, my stomach bloated with pain, making chitchat. I didn't begrudge people their reactions. It just surprised me. I couldn't say which was lonelier, living as a pastor's wife or being that wife in a disintegrating marriage.

The neighbors no longer waved to me when I pulled out of the driveway in my car. They no longer said, "Hi Wendy! How ya doin' today?" Our neighbors next door had a patio party; one friend in a lounge chair holding a beer; another slipping in and out of the back door. People I'd once chatted with easily in side yards and garden plots. I went to the back to water my flowers, putting me within spitting distance of the merriment. No one acknowledged me.

One of the saddest pictures during this early stage is remembering how I'd walked across the grassy field near our home, returning from the bank. I'd just opened a separate bank account with a hundred dollars remitted to me from my son in repayment for a speeding ticket. It was 90 degrees and the field grass stuck to my legs. My purse hung crossways across my shoulder, and I carried awkwardly the plastic Rubbermaid step stool/tool box tote, my "free gift" for opening the account. I remember thinking, *I have a hundred dollars in the bank and a plastic step stool tool box tote.*

I am left to cobble together imperfect illustrations of what these moments felt like by recalling various incidents around this time. An episode occurred a few months prior to the filing, that, looking back seemed a portent. I was pruning a bush in our front yard when in the snap-snap-snapping, I felt something that seemed more sinewy than a branch. A mourning dove lighted from the bush, dropping to the ground, incapacitated, flapping her damaged wings in a desperate and futile attempt to take flight. She hobbled across the street into a neighbor's yard. I called my (then) eighteen-year-old son Jon (the only son still at home) and together we searched that yard for the stricken bird. We never found her.

After that, Jon finished the pruning. He was hacking away when a branch dropped to the ground in which he found a nest holding a downy baby mourning dove. Jon said, "You killed its mother."

"I killed its mother!" I reeled.

Already stricken with the thought of the damaged bird dying alone somewhere in the neighbor's yard, now I stared benumbed at the orphaned nestling.

"I'll get milk!" I said.

Jon responded with typical dispassion: "Birds don't drink milk. They eat worms."

We named the baby bird Maynard and settled him into a box, wrapping him in towels and socks. I dug three fat worms from the back garden and brought them to Jon, who tried feeding them to Maynard. But Maynard wouldn't eat. "That's because baby birds eat only partially digested worms their mothers eat and bring back up," he said. "And since you injured and probably killed the mother, it has no partially digested worms to eat. Maybe you should take the worms and chop them up so they'll be almost as good as partially digested worms."

"I simply can't do that. You just have to accept it," I said.

Later that day, Jon came to me. "The birds are mad at us. I feel a lot of negative energy coming from them." He was correct, of course. The birds were mad at us that day. More to the point, they were mad at me. I'd killed one of them, a mother in its nest.

That's what it felt like when my neighbors turned away, and when help with a garage sale could not be found. The desperation and futility of that hobbled mother bird trying to regain flight after I had mutilated her, offered an apt, if ironic, picture of my own desperation and futility carrying the Rubbermaid step stool/tool box tote across the dry grassy field that sweltering day. Maynard, his searching beak tilted now this way, now that, hoping for food from his mother, was the picture of my helplessness catching the drift that our pastor friend did not intend to rise with a hug.

Maynard's mother had been the only terms he'd known for survival in this world. But I had killed her and now he was helpless. Maynard would not be saved without some other terms, outside intervention, terms he could not dictate or control. It came to me dimly, in these small disorienting moments, that I too would not be saved except by terms beyond my reach and control.

That September, as the first stages of the Dark Night cast early shadows, between bouts of stomach trouble and sleepless nights, I'd been reading in the psalms. One stood out because it reminded me of Maynard: "Open your mouth wide, and I will fill it with good things."[1] I didn't know what this could mean. Maynard had opened his mouth wide, but his source of predigested worms had been taken away. He opened his little mouth and there was no mother to fill it, at least in terms he understood.

I wondered what was one to *ask for* when opening one's mouth wide. Even if I knew what I wanted to ask for, how would I know I was asking for the right thing? What if I opened my mouth wide, asked wrongly — not knowing how to ask aright — and received no filling? What if after opening, asking, wondering, and receiving no filling, I lost hope?

My known world was being swept away in a rushing river. My praying felt hollow. So much of my understanding of God, my sense of his intimate acquaintance and participation in his activity, had been predicated upon prayer. Not only prayer but the sense that it *means something* when I pray; that such acquaintance and intimacy affects something. My world had broken apart. I'd fallen into the breach. I felt my prayers had failed.

God, presumably, was in his heavens. But I'd concluded he had his own way of doing things and wasn't interested in input from me. Still, I kept praying, I can't say why. I didn't believe these prayers would be acted upon — maybe sympathetically doted over — but not resulting in an effectual change. It seemed at the time rather a kind of relaxation exercise, like rhythmic breathing, that humored everyone — God, Jesus, me — everyone. We sat there, all of us, the picture of repose as I prayed and prayed and prayed and I'd hear them whisper, *She's pathetic.* I didn't mind. I was pathetic.

Where does one go after exerting trust in prayer and finding disaster?

⌘

The good news, according to the gospel writers, begins with John standing in a river, bringing bad news: "The ax of God's judgment is poised, ready to sever your roots. Yes, every tree that does not produce good fruit will be chopped down and thrown into the fire."[2] People came from cities and towns to hear it — city people, coming to the wilderness. Was it for the spectacle? Was it for a second chance? What did John possess that they so craved?

Jesus asked the same question: "Who is this man in the wilderness that you went out to see? Did you find him weak as a reed, moved by every breath of wind? Or were you expecting to see a man dressed in expensive clothes? . . . Were you looking for a prophet?"[3]

He says, "From the time [of John] until now, the Kingdom of Heaven has been forcefully advancing."[4] What kind of personality could bring forceful advancement of a spiritual kingdom by rendering bad news? Good news often arises out of bad news, and so it was with me. My journey began like Mark's gospel, with the ax. The good news is, it resulted in the forceful advancement of a spiritual kingdom amid the wreckage of my life. But only after the ax.

A young woman named Franny, in J. D. Salinger's *Franny and Zooey,* had been driven to near despair with life's superficialities and betrayals. "All I know is I'm losing my mind," she says. "I'm just sick of ego, ego, ego. My own and everybody else's. I'm sick of everybody that wants to *get* somewhere, do something distinguished and all, be somebody interesting. It's disgusting — it is, it *is.* I don't care what anybody says."

This incited in her a desire to pray. Yet Franny did not know how to pray. That is, until she latched onto a little book called *The Philokalia,* which espoused the spiritual benefits of repeating the "Jesus Prayer." She clung to the book tenaciously and explained to her skeptical lover:

[I]t starts out with this peasant — the pilgrim —
wanting to find out what it means in the Bible when it
says you should pray incessantly. You know. Without
stopping. In Thessalonians or someplace. . . . Then he
meets this person called a starets — some sort of terribly advanced religious person — and the starets tells
him about a book called the "Philokalia." Which
apparently was written by a group of terribly advanced
monks who sort of advocated this really incredible
method of praying. . . .

Well, the starets tells him about the Jesus Prayer
first of all. "Lord Jesus Christ, have mercy on me." I
mean that's what it is. And he explains to him that
those are the best words to use when you pray.
Especially the word "mercy," because it's such a really
enormous word and can mean so many things. . . .[5]

She said praying this way had a "really tremendous mystical
effect on your whole outlook," as if something was supernaturally
appropriated in repetitive praying. I saw the transaction implied by
the word "mercy." To pray "have mercy" suggests that for the petitioner there are no names to drop, nor anything to bring, no hopes
or dreams, no claim to stake, no honor to defend, no project or plan
or intent to explain. Only nakedness and madness or queerness,
things that typify the human predicament. Fatigue perhaps, perhaps
regret, perhaps collapse, that is all. It is opening one's mouth wide
and asking for nothing, waiting to receive whatever is given.

Jesus asked city people, What did you go to the wilderness to see? A prophet? A locust-eating freak? Maybe they hoped for a second chance. In any case, they went to see a man named John and stumbled onto something they had not been looking for. Their journey turned on them. Instead of hailing a delivering prophet, they discovered a peculiar man, a bearded eccentric who spoke bad news about axes being laid and fruits showing repentance. The real journey for those seekers began the way my journey began for me, in inhospitable territory where terms of survival are surrendered. Only One can bring about a rescue. I, like Maynard, opened my mouth hoping for something while asking for nothing, willing to take whatever was fed me, if only I might live. It was as mysterious and inauspicious as that.

***

We tried feeding Maynard chopped worms (Jon did), alas, to no avail. I held the little bird in my palm and stroked his downy, bony back. I spoke to him in reassuring tones, the way a mother would speak to a baby. I spoon-fed him warmed oatmeal with a little sugar. He latched his little beak to the spoon and siphoned the gruel, bit upon bit.

I knew the time had come to take Maynard to the animal shelter when he began to think of me as his mother. On the third day after we'd pulled him from the nest, I walked into Jon's room to speak to my son. Upon hearing my, by now, familiar voice, Maynard squeaked and squawked and flailed his little wings in an effort to make his way out from the socks. He was greeting me. My voice and presence had evidently left its mark.

The people at the shelter expressed surprise that Maynard had eaten oatmeal from a spoon. How odd, it seemed, that this little bird had attached itself in complete trust to the one who'd snapped the wings of its mother.

And so, that September, when the divorce papers were filed, the friends stopped calling, the neighbors stopped waving, the one I thought would be pastoral made an obvious retreat. The descent began. The ax had been laid. The picture had changed. A voice arose in the wilderness that changed the terms of survival, the summons of a locust-eating freak. Maynard was not given predigested worms from the mouth of his mother. He was given oatmeal from a cold metal spoon. But he was helpless. He took it.

When I thought of how it was supposed to be in the Christian life, in relationship to how it ended up being, the thought occurred to me, *This isn't how I pictured it.* Still, I quickly understood there was no place to go but where the hand that fed me led me. God first led his people, Israel, into the wilderness as part of their deliverance from Egypt. They were tested there. In the wilderness they, and I, were forced to decide whether to abandon humanly concocted devices and follow him truly, blindly, into the dark, or whether to stay safe in old habits and familiar routines even if it meant returning to bondage in Egypt.

My descent began in September. Shadows closed in. Where could I go? Whom else should I follow? I will follow you, even if on broken legs.

CHAPTER TWO

BLESS THE MUNDANE

I received a phone call during this time from a Nigerian man who resided in the United States and was attending my husband's church. He spoke with that African-British lilt that disarmed and at the same time lent authority. He said, "God asked me to speak to you."

He asked if I had a Bible. Then he asked me to turn to the book of Ephesians, chapter one, which I did. He said, "Would you read verse seventeen? And I will read verse eighteen."

I read: "I pray for you constantly, asking God, the glorious Father of our Lord Jesus Christ, to give you spiritual wisdom and understanding, so that you might grow in your knowledge of God." He read: "The eyes of your understanding being enlightened; that ye may know what is the hope of his calling, and what [are] the riches of the glory of his inheritance in the saints."[1]

He asked if he could pray for me. "Father," he said, "I thank you for the words you have spoken to us today, that we may know the hope of your calling. I do not know much about my sister. I know she is a writer, that's all. I ask you to bring your kingdom down because we pray 'Thy kingdom come.'

"Father," he said, "it is the ninth month of the year. Every month of the year you are doing miracles. May your miracles not be lost this month."

That man's prayer stayed with me: "Bring your kingdom down. May your miracles not be lost this month." Those words became as a clanging bell in a dark sea.

In happier days when I'd claim life's miracles, I'd go to my patio, a haven of beauty and tranquillity and hilarity as I watched little creatures go about their daily missions. That fall my patio was silent. I swept it only when a prospective house buyer came along. The drone of cicadas haunted me. My petunias had died, my little friend Chippy the chipmunk having eaten them. I forgave him. What else could I do? Nevertheless, he'd ruined my petunia patch, so I gave up on it and pulled them up and planted mums so something would fill in the dirt, in an attempt to sell the house. I didn't think Chippy would like mums. I thought they'd be too stiff and mealy for his tastes. I didn't care for mums. I'd never planted them before. I'd stopped putting water in my Mexican fountain because it sat unused. Standing water bred mosquitoes. What with the West Nile virus going around, who needed more mosquitoes?

I was not of a mind to see miracles during these days.

Maynard had taught me to open wide my mouth, without terms, and take what is given. Another episode occurred that fall that brought the Nigerian man's prayer strangely alive, steadied my feet to make the descent, and grounded me in everyday miracles.

Friends of mine who were taking a trip had asked me to stay a few days with their daughters. I'll call them Caitlin and Ali (then 11 and 8). One of those days happened to fall upon the same day the divorce papers were filed in county court. The girls were in school. I drove to the courthouse, remitted the papers, received a "case number," set the court date, walked back to my car, and felt the earth rock under me.

Even so, Caitlin had to be picked up at 11:30 and it was 11:10. On top of that I needed to stop by my house to pick up some things, and my house was on the opposite side of town. I would get Caitlin first, I thought, and have just enough time to drive to my house, retrieve my things, and make it back in time to pick up Ali at a different school at 12:15.

As I write, I do not remember "the things" I felt so anxious to recover. I remember only how badly I needed them and how that thought, after my responsibilities to the demands of the girls' sched-ules, drove my will. I imagine, more than "the things" themselves (whatever they were) I was needing to reconnect to the place I'd called home. That day — the day my marriage became a case number — I craved a reminder that I'd had a home and that my things were there and that I could go get them and touch them and have them with me when I felt the need. My "things," I thought, would tether me amid the rolling earth beneath me. Even as I waited for Caitlin a block from her school, I could not feel where I was, or the ground I stood upon.

Caitlin made it to my car fifteen minutes late. Her backpack had gotten jammed in her locker three times. Her friend Cassandra was with her, tumbling into the back seat behind Caitlin. A curly haired, freckled girl with the look of a Peanuts comic-strip character, Cassandra pleaded through narrow lenses of oval glasses, "I need you to sign this so I won't get a detention." She said she'd asked the teacher if it was all right for me to sign it and the teacher said it was. So I signed it, though I didn't know what I was signing and before this moment had never laid eyes on Cassandra. I was anxious to get going. Before I could pull out, however, Cassandra shuffled more papers from her Trapper Keeper and started scribbling. She said this had to be turned in by 2:00 or she would get yet another detention.

"Is that homework, Cassandra?" I asked. She looked at me queerly. "We'll get you back here before 2:00. Just go hand in that other sheet, the one I just signed."

By this point it was 11:50 and I desperately needed to get my things before picking up Ali at 12:15. Cassandra ran dutifully, sensing my nervousness, for which I commend her. In the meantime, Caitlin assured me we could be a few minutes late getting Ali because once her dad was an hour late picking her up, which didn't console me. Cassandra returned and I pulled away, hoping against hope not to be stuck behind a train on our way to the other side of town. Then Cassandra said, "Are we going home to have lunch now?" Caitlin had told me Cassandra was diabetic and had to eat at certain specific times, otherwise she'd pass out, but she — meaning Caitlin — knew what to do if that happened. I abandoned all thoughts of retrieving my things. I took Caitlin and Cassandra home so Cassandra could eat. (She promptly shoved a leftover pancake into her mouth.) I left to pick up Ali.

I felt oddly settled during this, the second school pickup. I had almost forgotten that the county court was this very day processing papers that would end life as I knew it. Ali was gleeful approaching my car, her clipped blonde locks bouncing in the wind. Trusting that Cassandra's diabetes had been controlled, I returned apace to the other side of town to retrieve my things.

And there they were, just as I'd left them, in a bag by the door.

By the time we returned — Cassandra was fine — Cassandra's 2:00 homework deadline loomed and I had to get her back to the school to hand in her assignment. Ali thought it a good idea to deliver the Michigan cherry pie she and I'd made the previous night, keeping up with her recent money-making pie-baking business, since, she said, "We're going out anyway."

"Good idea," I said and grabbed the pie. Ali joined Caitlin and Cassandra, waiting in the car. We delivered the pie and still made it to the school before 2:00, all of us awash with relief that Cassandra would not have detention.

But no. The front door was locked. Cassandra asked me to take her to the back door, which I did, but it too was locked. Cassandra's hopes of going to the mall quickly faded, thinking now she'd have to go to detention instead. Both schools doors were locked and it was nearly 2:00. I said I'd write her a note. Why not? I'd already signed something and her teacher had said it was okay. Caitlin then came up with the brilliant idea to knock on Mrs. Somebody's window. Cassandra's hopes alighted, yet she didn't want to be so daring on her own. Caitlin accompanied her in solidarity. They disappeared behind the building while Ali and I waited in suspense. Five minutes later they returned in a flush of excitement. Naseem had let them in. Naseem! That ragamuffin who never did his homework and so always had detention! He was more than happy to rescue the desperate Cassandra, who now rejoiced because she could go to the mall and would not have to go to detention.

Winded, but satisfied, Caitlin said, "And who do you have to thank?"

Cassandra said, "Oooooo, thank you, Caitlin!"

<hr />

Later that day as the girls played a rousing game that included an American Girl doll named Samantha, I settled into the solace of my room and read in the psalms. *He calms the storm to a whisper. What a blessing that stillness is.*[2]

"Uh — hello, Samantha," I heard Cassandra say. She brought me the doll, now decapitated, and handed its head to me. "I was fixing her hair and pulled off her head," she said. I told her I'd work on it.

The doll's head lay lifelessly on the floor. So sad, Samantha's eyes fixed, half shut, her smile unmoved, her hair balled up and ratted. Cassandra hadn't done well with your hair, dear; certainly not worth losing one's head over. *Jerusalem is a well-built city. Here stand . . . the thrones of the dynasty of David. Pray for the peace of Jerusalem.*[3]

I put the head back on. It wasn't hard. Sometimes Samantha's hair got in the way of the neck connection. But she survived. Her eyes opened again.

Other than managing Cassandra's near disasters that first day, the weekend with the girls settled down, and for a brief reprieve my world stopped rocking. I made their lunches and helped with homework. We chatted about Britney Spears, who'd recently broken up with Justin Timberlake, which Ali thought sad. "They liked each other. But she was afraid he was going to ask her to marry him."

I said, "Did you know that if you rearrange the letters in Britney Spears' name it spells Presbyterians?"

Ali looked at me. "What are those?"

We watched *Honey, I Shrunk the Kids.* Caitlin thought they should have gotten a cuter guy to play the boy who kisses the girl. Ali said, "He's cute." Caitlin said, "He's pathetic." They both cried when Anty, the baby ant, got killed by the scorpion, so we fast-forwarded that part. Ali made me a cootie-catcher: paper folded symmetrically into triangular cones that open and shut with hidden messages folded inside. We did the color-picking, finger-moving, paper-unfolding thing, and Ali told me my fortune: "You will get a big-screen TV."

"Wow," I said.

"It's not true," said Ali.

"I know."

"Well, it may be," she said.

"You never know," I said.

"But one day you will know."

<hr>

A final challenge arose, however, our last day together, when the girls wanted to go to church. I hadn't been inside a church for many months. Church triggered too much pain, the smell of the bulletin, the angle of the pews, the chitchat between worshipers before the music began.

The girls primped their hair and carried little purses. Caitlin carried her Bible and Ali brought her shiny pink diary with three hearts and a gold lock on the cover. We sat in the pew, I in the middle, and I felt at once lost at sea and buoyed by the two little girls flanking me. The long-haired sultry one to my left drew elephant faces on the visitor's register; the younger little blonde firecracker wrote furiously in her diary.

I listened to the sermon with that upward tilt of the chin, a posture perfected by pastors' wives. At some point the pastor lost a page of his manuscript and had to glance at the overhead to see what came next. "Christians have happier marriages than nonChristians," he said. "They have happier families, they make a thousand dollars a month more than nonChristians, and have better sex. Talk about frosting on the cake?" He was kidding. He said this kind of thinking deludes us into believing we control our comfort levels.

Then he said, "I'm a pastor; I'm paid to be good," and people laughed. Ali folded her dollar from the tooth fairy and pressed it neatly into a little white envelope, carefully licked and sealed it, waiting to drop it in the offering plate. She tapped my elbow to show me her diary. "Dear Diary, I love you. I just started writing in you." She hadn't noticed the wetness in my eyes.

"In God's kingdom there is something better than feeling good," the pastor said in his sermon, and I couldn't say what in God's kingdom was better than feeling good. I didn't see the humor in his joke. All the paychecks in the world couldn't put back my lost marriage to a pastor. I wasn't "feeling good." I didn't know if that meant I was close to the kingdom of God.

"Bring your kingdom down," my Nigerian friend had prayed. Ali was drawing a picture of Jesus in her diary. She wrote, King of

Heaven over his head. She added, "Jesus, seeing exactly how he is, loved him."

"Great misfortunes are monotonous," wrote Albert Camus in his novel *The Plague.* One of the more unsettling aspects of this journey was being consciously aware of devastation rolling over my life, while I filled my time with trivialities. Yet I came to see these as God's miracles, the answer to my Nigerian friend's prayer.

On the day the earth rocked beneath me, I saved Cassandra from two detentions, a diabetic blackout, and near-disaster with an American Girl doll. Ali and I delivered a Michigan cherry pie. We overcame Anty's being eaten by the scorpion and got Presbyterians out of Britney Spears. When I had no will or strength to move myself, little moments in common places were, in a way, God's kingdom coming down. His miracles alighted from unexpected angles.

I ordered a Michigan cherry pie from Ali's pie-baking business to send to my sons at college. I paid extra for a personal note from Ali. She wrote, "I hope you like it" — meaning the pie. Then, turning the card to its back side, she wrote, "You gotta take what comes."

It was the ninth month of the year. Father, every month of the year you are doing miracles. May your miracles not be lost this month. May we finish our work and get it in on time. May the eyes of our understanding be enlightened. May we recapitate headless dolls. May we not lose hope, even if we don't win the big-screen TV. May we love the way Jesus loved, seeing exactly how we are. May King of Heaven be written over our heads. May we love as Ali loves her diary. May we understand hope when the earth rocks beneath us, and know that there are miracles every day to hold on to. May we believe that one day we will know. In the meantime, may we take what comes.

CHAPTER THREE

ENTER THE CHAOS

By mid-October, balmy vestiges of summer had turned to bitter portents of winter. Laden cloud cover erased shadows and monotonous gray overtook the landscape. Trees and birds grew agitated. Coldness and darkness changed the picture of my surroundings and the locus of my inner journey too. With the divorce papers filed and the house on the market, my tethers to the "ordinary" were thinning out. This part of the journey entailed tedious waiting.

Frederick Buechner had said life was either a black comedy or it was a mystery, and it didn't feel like a black comedy. It felt like a mystery,' and mine was a mystery indeed. Sometimes my face would burn and my lips would throb, my nostrils would swell and my throat constrict. Tears always puddled on the edges of my eyes. Whatever the weather or my inner condition, I took my daily walks. I'd find myself saying, "Where am I?" I'd lose my bearings and forget where I was on the path. I could only plod on with dull endurance, a wet wind in my face.

Once I passed by a local elementary school during recess. Have you ever really listened to the sound of children playing on a playground at recess? These children did nothing at low decibels. They screamed. They howled. They hooted. They ran around like maniacs.

It felt as if I'd wandered into a country where a "pandemonium of fairy devils . . . seemed to have suddenly assembled about me."[2] It was chaos, and it brought to mind a conversation my youngest son Jon and I had shared before he left for college. He told me about a rock band he liked because, he said, "they intentionally mess around with chaos." They were so confident in themselves as musicians, he said, "that right when you think their songs are becoming chaotic, they bring them into order."

Perhaps that is why I walked. Maybe I feared the chaos was gaining the upper hand and I was trying to bring it into some kind of order.

***

Despite feeling hopeless and purposeless in it, I would kneel before God in spiritual poverty. I felt bewildered, not knowing how to pray, but continued at times against my will, because I'd surrendered the terms of my survival. There were many times I'd have preferred not to have prayed, to have stayed in the warmth of my bed. I'd make myself rise, tired and chilled, then I'd kneel. I'd state up front I didn't know what to say or how to pray or what to pray for. If Jesus is honest and sane, as I'd concluded he was; if his assumptions about prayer could be trusted, to which I had so concurred; then his example of praying seemed the model to undertake. I kept telling myself, I will not go mad.

"We see him there, a kneeling Figure," writes George Buttrick of Jesus in the Garden of Gethsemane. "He is silhouetted now against the wheel of stars. The silver wheel slowly turns, but he still kneels. . . . Is he speaking now as if God were on the other side of that ledge of rock? Does the sky ever seem brassy to him, his only answer an echo? . . . We hear words, 'Thy will . . . Thy will.'"[3]

But how does one pray thy will, thy will, and mean it?

⁕

"To take chaotic unassociated ideas or events and make order is a holy act," Jon had said in that discussion about the rock band. "Chaos is a way God reveals himself in disparate parts. It helps break him apart into smaller, more manageable pieces," he said. "The ultimate expression of bringing chaos into order is the Cross."

What did Jesus mean when he said, "My flesh is the true food and my blood is the true drink. All who eat my flesh and drink my blood remain in me"?[4] Whatever he meant, it was "a hard teaching" and he lost many followers as a result.[5] He said, "If you remain in me and my words remain in you, you may ask any request you like and it will be granted."[6]

If remaining in him implied, to some degree, eating his flesh and drinking his blood, and if this teaching was hard enough to turn away would-be followers, wouldn't it suggest that "remaining" (whatever it is) must also be hard? The Cross, my son had said, "is the most extreme chaos and the most extreme order manifested in a single event." Can things of earth meet the fullness of heaven? Can eating and drinking his flesh and blood — bread and wine — bring this about?

It demands a surrender of human understanding, just as in the broken body of Christ, God surrenders his God-ness. God cloaked in blood; it is a mystery. His brokenness becomes ours somehow. In eating and drinking his flesh and blood, our brokenness becomes his. I came to understand the logic this way: If the wood and nails remain in you, and you remain in them, then ask what you will, and it will be done for you. I began to understand that the only way through the chaos was to pray thy will, thy will, the prayer of wood and nails.

So I prayed as Jesus had prayed. I didn't know if I was praying aright or if the words I spoke even found a hearing. More than once I arose from my bed with a sense that I'd lost the battle. Hope had left me. Having a "quiet time" with God only bewildered me. Words in the Bible were meant to inspire hope and instill courage: "Be strong and of good courage, do not fear . . . for the LORD your God, He is the One who goes with you."[7] The words left me cold. I did not want to read promises about hope and courage. I felt no sense of his presence, and God knows I had no strength. Aching, groping, thrashing, stumbling into forward leans, yes. Good? Courage? My life contradicted them. I could see nothing good, nor could I feel anything like courage. My stomach was collapsing in on itself, and I was confused enough already.

I had read that an old monastic was asked once, "What do you do in the monastery all day?" He said, "Oh, fall down and get back up." I kept falling down, kept finding my knees to the carpet. I fell often and hard until I finally understood that the carpet is where God met me, rug burns to the knees. For all God's power and transcendence, the carpet was where he met with me.

That fall, a dream I had made the chaos more clear. In it, I'd gone to France on vacation and the place where I stayed was a hostel, but it seemed more like a cathedral, with high vaulted ceilings and deep wooden paneling. Instead of sightseeing, I chose to remain in the hostel to join a choir that was assembling in the cathedral-like main room. The tune of the song we sang was remotely familiar, though I did not know the words because they were in French. There were no notes on the pages so I depended upon others in the choir to help get the pronunciation and rhythms right. Of the two choir directors in the dream, the first emphasized the need to sing the song over and over again. I can still hear a soprano singing, repeating her aria. I still hear myself singing my part. I'd mastered the rhythms because of the repetition. Sometimes I strained to reach high notes, but in my dream I hit them and was not embarrassed. When the second choir director took over, his demands were more exacting. At the same time, he was more helpful in his assistance. He went much further than the first director in enabling me to understand the nuances of the rhythm.

Toward the end of the dream, the second director was preparing us for the performance. He said, "When you sing a masterpiece like this one, even if you don't understand the words, there is something it is trying to say. If you reach that level of perfection, it will say it."

Jon used to tell stories during his last two years of high school when he worked with the "special needs" students. (Local schools seem a microcosm of life in its rudimentary expressions.) He'd come home and recount in startling detail the thoughts or responses or bizarre interactions with Jana or Roger or Jake. In spite of an immoderate and chaotic environment, he spoke of these interactions with tenderness toward these damaged people, as if chaos itself was their gift.

Jana, he'd said, was less mentally disabled than the others and so was surrounded by people whose limitations surpassed her own. She was easily angered and frustrated in this environment, in part because she didn't know she was mentally disabled. She believed that when others in the class made her angry she actually "got stupider," as Jon put it indelicately. He described how one time Jana fell, hurt her knee, and felt angry, but she held it in "because," Jon said, "she feared getting dumber."

Roger was autistic. He clung tenaciously and inordinately to the gym teacher, Mrs. Watkins. He was so attached to her that when he spoke, he'd end each tortured comment with the word "Watkins-ah." If Jon asked him what he wanted to do, Roger might say, "Teach Jon a song Watkins-ah." If Jon asked Roger if he wanted to play a game, Roger would answer, "Yes-ah Watkins-ah."

Jake, also autistic, was "totally controlled by id," Jon said. He "ferociously grabbed other people's food and stuffed it into his mouth." Sometimes he made unrestrained and unwanted sexual advances to unsuspecting students in the hallway between classes ("great hormonal motivation with a weakness in expression," Jon said). Jake spoke only one word — a profanity beginning with *sh* — and he usually uttered it in a growl with obsessive finger twitching. "What I wonder is, since Jake *can* speak," Jon said, "why does he speak only in a noncommunicative anger-releasing manner?" One time Jake grabbed Jon by the hair and wouldn't let go. So Jon grabbed Jake by the hair. Jake pulled harder. So Jon pulled harder. They stayed locked in mutual hair pulling for several minutes, each holding the other without budging. Finally Jake let go. Then Jon let go.

I would tread familiar sidewalks, face to the wind, not knowing where I was except in the company of screaming children on wild playgrounds where there seemed no rules. It was the picture of my predicament: I was in a wilderness where the Devil prowled, a country of madness (as Thomas Merton called it). It was the same place the Spirit had driven Jesus: to the wilderness to confront the king of demons.

Maybe Jana's fear of becoming "stupider" when anger arose, and her efforts to beat it back, were her attempts to bring the chaos to order, the way Jesus confronted the Devil in the wilderness. Maybe chaos itself was his praying for me, the way Roger's ending every sentence with Watkins-ah was an amen to hope. Maybe Jake's *sh*-word, his screams and twitches, were his rebuke of chaotic forces pinning his id to a world from which he could not escape or give expression to short of a curse. Maybe it was his cry to be free, the way Jesus rebuked the Devil and made him flee. Maybe Jake's pulling Jon's hair was his attempt to hold on to something real and powerful, something to meet him in his wilderness. And maybe Jon pulling Jake's hair aroused Jake's trust, showing him he wouldn't let go, no matter how hard Jake pulled. Maybe Jake, understanding Jon wouldn't let go, felt safe enough to surrender the id and trust something outside himself.

"When you sing a masterpiece like this one, even if you don't understand the words, there is something it is trying to say." Maybe the twitches, obsessions, and even profanities of the special needs students were, each in its own way a masterpiece; the screams and howls of children on the playground, singing their parts over and over again without notes on the page; hoots and howls and growls and twitches reaching a kind of perfection, uttering what could not be expressed in mere words — prayers on the edges of chaos. Only the chaos could make them masterpieces.

"You guys, you guys, time out." A young girl on the playground that day, the pitcher for kickball, stopped the game. She held the ball under her arm, rallied the teams, and held a brief tribunal at home plate. This suggested that rules at some point came into play.

I'd walk, day after day, whatever the weather and regardless of aches or lack of sleep. One morning I walked a trail that wove between a grouping of baseball diamonds at a nearby park. I heard a *wreep-wreep-wreep,* the chirp of a cardinal I could not see. I looked up and around and there he was, perched on an upper branch of a blue spruce tree. The incandescence of his redness lent a stunning contrast to the icy blue of that tree. He sang and sang, and I stopped, alone in the bloom of an early morning at the center of a web of deserted baseball diamonds. Then I knew there were rules even amid chaos. Birds sing on high branches and pine trees point upward. Color and song and wind and wet fill the edges of earth's mysteries. It is a masterpiece that needs to be spoken despite words that are lost in translations.

There were times, in the chaos of this journey, when nothing made sense. I didn't know where I was or how I'd gotten there. Then there were other times, like that one, when the song of a bird high in a tree shocked my life to a standstill and I knew there were rules. The Sane and Honest One uttered *thy will, thy will* and was asking me to lay down my doubts and say it too. The only way out of the Dark Night was to follow him in. He must find me waiting in the space that was my space, my carpet. He'd meet me there, not as a sage or prophet, but as a fellow madman who'd already beaten down the chaos. I could not have won that battle had he not gone before me. "Let me be content with whatever darkness surrounds me, finding him always by me, in His mercy," Merton wrote.[8] He had me by the hair.

Winter

CHAPTER FOUR

FOLLOW THE SIGNS

⸎

I continued to wonder what, if anything, had been the measurable effect of the praying. For all my nightly vigils on my knees in silence, the house still hadn't sold. I was down to my last article assignment of the year, for which I'd already been paid, which meant I was out of money. I was being overtaken by incapacitating attacks in my stomach and had lost twenty-three pounds. That, and other related complexities, had caused me to conclude my praying affected little, at least in an immediate sense. The deeper into the chaos I went, the further away God's consolations seemed.

That November, the last article assignment would take me to Tuba City, Arizona. Shortly before I left, I spoke over the phone with Jon. I was catching him up: The house hadn't sold; there had been very little movement.

"Do you think that's a sign?" he asked.

I paused. "I don't believe in signs."

"Are you still a Christian?" he said.

I told Jon I was still a Christian, but that all "signage" of God's movements had left me. "Signs only tease," I said. "They rarely pan out." I'd once believed in signs, I said. In fact, I'd acted upon my belief in "signs." I saw it as an act of faith. Isn't that how Christians are supposed to live? But at the time when I told Jon I didn't believe in signs, things weren't panning out. So I stopped looking for signs. I resolved that if anything remotely resembling a "sign from God" came down from the heavens, I'd dismiss it. I would not act upon it.

At the time I'd been reading a little book about the "offices" of prayer, specific times of the day and night when a monastic community would stop what they were doing, take the breviary (a prayer manual), and read aloud prayers and Scriptures. It might take fifteen minutes. The office called *matins*, or the dark hours, were the early morning prayers spoken before dawn's light. The monks would gather and pray in silence by candlelight. The book said, "The shining flame lights up the things around it, but outside of this arbitrary circle of light lies deep darkness, which is limitless. That darkness is symbol and image for the divine mystery."[1]

Praying matins, the book said, was an invitation to "trust the darkness despite the immense fear it triggers." Praying matins teaches us to walk into the darkness and meet it. "We have to learn to meet mystery with courage that opens itself to life." When we do that, it said, "the very darkness shines."[2]

The assignment to Tuba City felt like that, like walking into darkness and meeting a mystery. The trip marked my first outing when I'd felt truly on my own. I had no one to call from the hotel room that night. No one to check in with. No one to anchor me to home back east. My house was for sale and when it sold I would be leaving. I did not know my place in this new world. It was a foreign land, counterintuitive and odd.

Tuba City, Arizona, was little more than a dusty crossroads on the Navajo reservation north of Flagstaff. Winding my way in a rented car through dry desert mountains, now and then my eye caught sight of canyon ridges and plateaus and pine forests. Sagebrush tumbled across the road before me. It felt like being in a movie.

The Painted Desert seemed an implausible contradiction: excruciating jagged stone ablaze in astonishing blushes of light. I thought it must have been God's Picasso phase during the creation.

When I started seeing hogans tucked into hollows of canyon ridges, I knew I was getting close. The sacred dwelling of the Navajo, the round "female" hogan faced east, toward the rising sun. The "male" hogan, a bundle of logs shaped like a teepee, reached skyward.

I'd come to meet a Navajo pastor I'll call Howard. His deep-toned roundish face seemed almost childlike given his age (eighty-five). He wore a Jesus Is Lord baseball cap as we met at a coffee shop later that day. He spoke in low tones. He told me he feared ill will of angry spirits who might overhear us. We were talking about Navajos who'd become Christians.

Howard told me about a friend of his, a one-time medicine man named Cloud Runner. Cloud Runner had once possessed unsurpassed healing powers, which provoked the envy of others in the same trade. Because of Cloud Runner's powers, the other medicine men had put a curse on him, Howard said. They sent messengers to harass him — coyotes wailed, and owls perched in the juniper trees outside his hogan. "When a medicine man makes contact with the spirit world he sends demons in an owl and it speaks to him in the Navajo way," Howard said. "Cloud Runner was hearing the owls say in the Navajo way, 'We are going to kill you — you — you.'"

The fear induced by the demon-owls would bring a curse upon the medicine man, his family, and his land, Howard said. And eventually, it would kill him. In fact, Cloud Runner's wife had fallen ill and his sheep were dying. He himself had been overtaken with an illness that threatened his life.

That was when Cloud Runner and his family attended a Christian gathering led by Howard. In desperation to stop the curse, he and his family went there to learn about the Great Chief whose power surpassed the incantations of medicine men. As Howard put it, Cloud Runner surrendered his land to the Great Spirit. Then Cloud Runner asked Howard how to get rid of the owls. Howard said, "Give them your testimony."

"The owls, like you and I," Howard continued in low tones, "have supernatural help." He said, "The psalmist says the angel of the Lord encamps round about those that fear him. We don't see them. But according to God's Word, I'm hedged around with angelic hosts. So are you."

I awoke the next morning at 4:00 AM after five hours of sleep. I decided to get up and drive — I didn't know where. *On the road.* That's as much as I knew. Maybe I would see a haunting sunrise on the Painted Desert.

I drove along a deserted road while the sun crept into its rising amid a thick layer of clouds. Alas, there was no sunrise to see. Cloud cover overtook the skies and the wind kicked up. After an hour or so, I turned back in order to make my morning appointment with Howard. As I neared the outskirts of Tuba City I saw a handwritten sign that read "Dinosaur Tracks" with an arrow pointing left. On a whim, I turned left down the unpaved rutted road. I'd never seen dinosaur tracks. I soon came upon an unoccupied makeshift vendor's shelter, which caused me to conclude the dinosaur tracks must be nearby. Then, not far from the shelter, I discovered another parked car. Stepping out of mine, I saw a man wandering around the barren landscape just beyond, his nose toward the ground. Obviously, he was looking for tracks.

I approached and he looked up. "I haven't seen any," he said. He was a handsome man, his salt-and-pepper beard suggesting he was about my age, and had a curious way about him. I wasn't sure how to interact. I looked down and saw tracks right away.

"Here's one." I pointed out a three-pronged footprint the size of a baseball mitt. He came to see. Then, between the two of us, we started seeing tracks all over the place.

"Wow, this one's really deep. Look at how long that gait is," he said. "Try stepping in it." I tried. He was right. It was a very long gait.

We walked about the desert landscape, this man and I, finding one huge footprint atop another, each one surpassing the previous in our collective astonishment. Down the path a ways we came upon a spot that looked like it could have been piles of petrified dung.

"This must have been their gathering place, you know, where they took their 'morning walk.'" He laughed. I did too.

He told me he had arisen early with hopes of seeing the same sunrise I'd wished for. Instead, we both ended up at the crack of dawn walking around the rocky desert where dinosaurs once walked and whose presence had been memorialized in petrified stone. He was a Christian, it turned out. He said he had "been through a lot of hard times." He added, "I'm going through a hard time right now."

I'd wanted to say, "You are? Why, *so am I*." But I held my tongue. He said the church he'd previously attended was "too driven by emotion."

"If emotion is your authority, that only brings you back to your-self," he said. "Look at this." He pointed. It was the biggest track we'd seen yet.

"Would you mind putting your foot next to that track for a picture? My son would love this. It will show the perspective." He complied happily. The track outsized the man's foot two times easily. His Birkenstock sandal and woolen socks proved a disarming contrast to the giant monster print impressed upon the rock.

"How's that?" he said. He extended his leg like a dancer.

"Perfect." I snapped the picture.

"I'll be on my way." He turned to leave. "Nice meeting you here." He nodded.

"I wish you well," I said. I never revealed to him that I had been "going through a hard time" myself. I suppose I hesitated to reckon with it, seeing as it was my first segue into life without my usual tethers. I imagine I felt afraid, and that telling him would cause him to pity me or lend solace, and that scared me too. I can't say why.

At his car, he turned and I waved good-bye. He looked up at the thickening clouds and the stirring winds. He said, "It's a gathering storm."

<hr>

I never learned his name. The only remembrance I possess of the man I met at the dinosaur tracks is the photo I took of his foot, a Birkenstock sandal in a fossilized track twice its size. I prayed God would help him through his hard time. I still pray for him.

My son had asked if I was still a Christian because I'd said I didn't believe in signs. What kinds of eyes do we need to see mysteries? Praying matins before sunrise allows hope that darkness itself can shine. I suppose that, in spite of myself, I believed in signs, or at least in the possibility that a sign might arise. Deciding to take that drive that morning — anywhere, somewhere — might have been the assertion of that hope. And a sign appeared. I made a quick left. I found my way to dinosaur tracks where a mysterious friend awaited me. We met on the desert at dawn. A thick sky overhead, fossilized earth at our feet, he lent his foot for my picture. I keep the photo at my desk. It helps me keep perspective.

Howard said I am hedged around with angelic hosts, and the way to dispel the curse of the demon-owls was to speak to them, give them a testimony. Cloud Runner returned to his hogan that night and said: "You owl people, you are trespassing, every one of you. In the name of the Great Chief, the Lord Jesus Christ, I command you to leave our place and never come back." Howard said, "one right after the other" the owls took flight.

Leaving the Painted Desert that day, I passed the sign that said "Dinosaur Tracks." I turned at the end of a road and then, like the stroke of a brush, the sun burst through a layer of clouds and shafts of light fell like fire on red clay. Sagebrush tumbled to higher ground. Clouds chased shadows and the junipers stirred. Light called forth beauty from jagged stone. Splendor met anguish. Heaven called earth, and earth itself became a shard of heaven, the way even the very darkness shines.

I was not afraid. The owl spirits had to leave because they were trespassing. The sign I saw when I'd made that quick left told me I was not alone even in desolate places, even amid a gathering storm.

CHAPTER FIVE

NOSE TO THE CARPET

I'd moved in this journey from a place of chaos to mystery. I'd been reading the portion of Scripture where David had said, "Worship the LORD in the beauty of holiness"[1] and wondered what he could possibly have meant by that. The immediate context had been the occasion of bringing the ark to Jerusalem, the City of David, to reside in the tabernacle. Did it suggest God's presence could be carried in a trunk capped with wings and brought to rest inside a tent? Anyway, how does bringing it there manifest worshiping "in beauty of holiness"? What is this beauty? How does "holiness" (whatever that is) express it?

To back up, answers to those prayers I prayed did come, if only through a back door. In the final days of November, we signed a contract on the house (to be out in three weeks). My dear friend and agent, a rock of safety and objectivity for me during this ordeal, left for a job on the West Coast. I learned my stomach pain had been caused by stones in my gallbladder. I got rear-ended in my car at a major intersection the day before my surgery. I underwent surgery to remove the gallbladder the Wednesday before Thanksgiving. My sons had left with their father to go out of state for the holiday, and I spent Thanksgiving day alone in bed recovering. The literature on laparoscopic gallbladder removal promised it "will make you feel good again. Best of all," it said, "you should still be able to live a full and happy life."

These were my answers, the violence it took to drive me to the innermost recesses of the Dark Night: Losing my agent, my beloved friend and needed support (not to mention the income he'd rustled up for me); getting hit from behind and knocked off course; getting my insides pulled out and bearing it alone. Who would go voluntarily? Losses, wreckages, stabbings, and displacement drive you there, down, down until there is no farther down to go. And there you are.

Two weeks later, in mid-December, I said good-bye to my husband. Two sons were back at school and the third, back to work. I spent the last night in my town in a Hampton Inn a mile from my house with an appointment to meet the judge the next morning. A character in Frederick Buechner's *Book of Bebb* novels, Antonio Parr is a sullen, middle-aged man who'd felt his share of blows in life and searched for meaning amid the wreckage. He said, "I have a feeling it's the in-between times, the time narratives like this leave out and that the memory in general loses track of, which are the times when souls are saved or lost."[2] That final morning was one of those times. I looked out the window of my hotel room at the Midwest flatlands, frost on the fields, barren trees, a silvery prairie, the scenery of my world. I'd come to the end of my life as I knew it. I looked out the window and heard myself say, "Where am I? I am in a Hampton Inn a mile from my house, looking at the prairie before I go to meet the judge."

That day in court my case number was summoned and I went before the bench alone. I don't remember much about it. I remember

I wore a red sweater and blue jeans (I would be driving to North Carolina as soon as it was over). I was alone because I couldn't afford a lawyer. I remember his gaze and dispassionate questions: "You're keeping your name?" (For my sons, I said.) "You can make a living by what you do?" No alimony was involved. (Yes sir, I said, though I didn't know whether I could or couldn't.) "You have no minor children?" (I wanted to say, minor? Of course they're not *minor* — they're *major!* I said, Yes, sir.)

He said this, he said that. I said something about having attended my husband's church for the last time in June, six months earlier. I don't know why it came up. He said something else, here and there, then he said, "The bonds of matrimony presently existing are hereby dissolved. Each of the parties is forever barred from claiming maintenance from the other, having waived the right thereto."

I left the courthouse and drove nine hours to North Carolina.

As far as places to be in mid-December, the basement apartment of my sister's home seemed best. Quiet and lovely, I could see the Blue Ridge mountains from the picture window and the beauty and mystery comforted me. My sister put out a small Christmas tree on a bookshelf there. Her daughter, my niece, made Christmas cookies from a family recipe. That was all I felt of Christmas that winter.

I continued to ponder "the beauty of holiness" and wondered what it could mean in my present context. I thought by now I'd know how to pray. But praying gave me headaches, and my stomach would turn. I'd light a candle and kneel in the dark, though it seemed the more I prayed the darker it got, save the candle flame. That, in any case, insisted on reaching upward. I felt dark inside myself. I thought about my sons, my ruined marriage, the friends lost through my move, and the trauma of our ordeal; about the weakness and fatigue and the ache that wouldn't go away. I thought, *How sad. How does one find holiness in this? Where could there be beauty in that holiness?* Then I'd hear inside myself, *Stop saying, "How sad." It's real. It's human. It's what happened.*

I was sometimes left in charge of the dog, Lucy, part chocolate Lab, part Boykin spaniel. The weekend my sister and her family went away, Lucy lay with me on my bed downstairs and I saw in her eyes what she must have seen in my eyes. Her family had gone away. She seemed lost, sad, tired, waiting. I regretted that I couldn't bring her more solace.

I'd pray in the dark with the candle as my focus. I'd stare at the light and sense that my longings were gathered in the flame. Darkness swallowed me except where that little light asserted itself. I felt my aching carried in the flame, as if Jesus lifted it and carried it further on, my Advocate. He knew what to do with it. He'd take it to the place it belonged where it would rest and stop saying, "how sad."

It was cold in that basement, so as I prayed, I'd pull a blanket over my head. Sometimes my feet got numb beneath me. Sometimes being on my knees didn't seem low enough. Then I'd bow, nose to the carpet, and hope my nieces didn't walk in. I'd feel movement, like horses galloping over me, like something riding high and fleet over something low, cheeks against the Berber. After a time I would rise to my knees, maybe more resolved, because I'd felt horses riding over me.

I didn't know what gave way when I prayed. Maybe that was the way it was meant to be — that I'd feel only numbness in my feet while the Holy One rides. I'd bow and he'd be there somewhere between the hair of my nose and the fiber of carpet. He was there, and sometimes it took falling down, to where an hour before Lucy had licked her haunches, to find him. It didn't occur to me to wonder when the vacuum was last run. Such thoughts evaporated when, face to the floor, the Holy One moved over me.

Worship the Lord in the beauty of holiness. My nose went down and I saw hands go up, lifting the blood, the cup of blessing. I was remembering an event that occurred a few years back in Ecuador. I'd accompanied a group of fifteen teens and five adult leaders on a mission project in the jungle town called Shell. The event occurred the morning we attended a small local church called Iglesia Luz del Evangelio (Light of the Gospel). We sat on wooden pews under wobbling ceiling fans and fluorescent lights, clay pots with artificial flowers adorning concrete-block walls. The windows had no screens. All manner of flying insects made their entrance. We sat shoulder to shoulder. Human smells were the sweet aroma of worship that day.

Nearing the conclusion of the service, elders of the church began to distribute the elements for communion, watered down grape juice and bite-sized Ritz crackers. About two-thirds of the way through the dispensing, the tray holding the little cups of "wine" ran out. I thought there was no cause for alarm. They'd return to the front and pick up another tray. It didn't take long to realize, however, there was no filled tray to retrieve. Like the wedding at Cana, the party had run out of wine. The musicians deftly kept playing. The serving had stopped two rows in front of where I sat. I had greatly anticipated *La Cena del Señor* (Lord's Supper). It was the one portion of the service that didn't involve a language barrier.

But they ran out of wine. They had no reserves. The worship team kept playing. The elders carried the empty trays, walking up and down the aisles, not sure what to do. At some point the bread came along, mini-Ritz crackers on a tray. I prepared myself to partake only of the bread, which was better than nothing at all.

Then I started seeing arms go up. In the front of the congregation people were lifting their hands, holding high their cups of watered down juice. They were wanting to put them back on the tray for the elders to distribute to those who were without. I don't know how many people raised their cups and returned them to the tray. Enough that there was a sufficient supply of grape juice for all to partake. Some shared the cup with their neighbor.

By the time the pastor gave the charge to "eat" and "drink," the elders were surrendering their little cups back to the tray so the music team could partake. It felt like the multiplying of the loaves and fishes.

What is beauty? Holiness? One knows it when one sees it. What happened in that little church that morning could not be called "beauty" in the sense that the episode had been "pretty." The kids in our group were bored witless (the service was in Spanish); the pews made our backs ache; the smell of body odor tightened our throats; bugs crawled about the shoulders of worshipers seated nearby. Yet if ever I perceived what it meant to worship God in the beauty of his holiness it was in that church during the odd moment when hands went up to give back communion cups. It made me want to weep, not for sorrow but for mystery. It was an ordinary thing, little cups put back on a tray. But God came down in that ordinary thing. A hand rises and God descends. A nose goes to the carpet, and he rises in a flame. David carried God's presence in a trunk into a tent.

Sometimes the candle flame faded, just like that. One minute it would rise like an opera singer. The next it would shrink in retreat, like a hunchback. The light would dim, perhaps to remind me that no matter how great the darkness, even if I was swallowed in darkness, the lowest flame could lead the way out. I thought it might be that my eyes grew dim, that my mind was telling me the flame only appeared to be fading. Anyway, it sheared the night. It scattered the hold darkness had on me.

My prayers were answered whether I saw or not. Whether I *got* what it was I thought I was praying for. Facedown like that, you're not praying *for* anything. You're thankful for movement enough to bring you back to your knees.

***

On New Year's Eve, the last day of that devastating year, I was alone in my sister's home. Lucy had been consigned to the basement with me, my fellow refugee. I lingered in bed just to feel her warmth. Tomorrow would be a different year, I thought. Maybe a new beginning for me.

Maybe this, maybe that. Life was full of maybes. I resolved not to think in terms of what might be, but only in terms of what was.

Sometimes I sensed all the praying in the world wouldn't free me from this prison. Those were the terms: I was pinned to earth.

Then a hand raised a cup and shared a promise. Horses rode over me, nose to the carpet. Something happened. A transaction took place. The situation began to turn itself.

Worshiping God in the beauty of holiness comes in little things that add up to a big thing, a cosmic thing. Our lives are the meeting ground. You get there by being hit from behind, knocked off course, by getting your insides pulled out. Laparoscopic gallbladder removal would make me feel good again and, best of all, *I'd be able to live a full and happy life.*

But not before going down till my nose met the Berber, dirt against my cheeks at the heartbeat of it. There, terms change and horses ride. It takes everything out of you and at the same time puts everything back in. You weep for the mystery of it. Lucy licked my face while I prayed. The holiness of it shook me. Those are the terms. Earth is the hammer of heaven.

CHAPTER SIX

TRAMPLE THE DESPAIR

𝒴ou are driven to the Dark Night by wreckages, down, down until there is no farther down to go. There you are. There you stay.

It was January's end. While I was thrashing about inside myself amid the chaos, mystery, holiness, and in an odd way, beauty of the Dark Night, I was also filling my days with thoughts of setting up the home I was soon to acquire. It was not far from where my sister lived (more on that later), but far away enough to maintain a degree of independence. The builder's name was Bill; we called him Bill the Builder, a chatty, happy man who took pride in his work and took his good time getting it right. The carpet man was Darrie; the tile man, Ernie; the Realtor was Rosie; and Stacy was the mortgage manager. Rosie, Stacy, Ernie, Darrie, and Bill: the poetry of my new life. My sister bought me many little things in preparation for my move: a laundry basket, an Oneida saucepan, measuring cups from the Dollar Store. She and I had animated discussions about grout; she's an expert on it and gave me sound helpful advice. She's also a math whiz who made graph paper layouts of my few pieces of furniture so I could fit them, like a puzzle, into the 1,260 square feet that would become my little home.

We were shopping one day and I bought a colander and a

cast-iron coat rack for thirty-three dollars. I was giddy over the find. For one hour, maybe two, a colander and coat rack erased fears and sorrows and insanities. Pondering a colander (smallish, mottled sage-green ceramic), I did not think about my life that had died. My sister walked each step with me and helped pick out my new accoutrements. She carried each burden with me, rejoicing with me at the colander find, her assertion that she would not let me die. I ached for her, wishing to lighten her load.

The best I could do, day in and day out, was render obedience to color-coded lists on my darkly comedic pen-and-ink illustrated appointment calendar: Edward Gorey's (1925–2000) "Neglected Murderesses." Sprinkled throughout weeks and months he depicted historical women driven to madness, who'd committed weird crimes. Red in my color coding denoted birthdays; purple, writing deadlines; green, travel and/or visitors; sky blue — oops, I mean "tarheel blue" — library book due dates; indigo, general engagements; pink, bills (it softened the blow).

In January, when in 1936 "Miss Q. P. Urkheimer brained her fiancé after failing to pick up an easy spare at Glover's [Bowling] Lanes, Poxville, Kansas," my color-filled day read like this:

· (Indigo)	BEST BUY modem self-installation kit
· (Indigo)	DRIVER'S LICENSE
· (Indigo)	FAX health insurance application
· (Indigo)	Copy proof of purchase receipts
· (Pink)	Pay Visa
· (Pink)	Pay Verizon

- (Pink)   Pay Association dues
- (Pink)   Pay BellSouth
- (Pink)   Pay Blue Cross and Blue Shield
- (Pink)   Pay Midwest Pathology (gallbladder)
- (Pink)   Pay hospital (gallbladder)
- (Pink)   Pay for ultrasound (gallbladder)

There was little marked in green (visitors). No tarheel blue. Mostly pink.

The following month, when Natasha Batti-Loupstein "pulverized a paste necklace and sprinkled it over a tray of canapés" in Villa Libellule, Nice (1923), the list read:

- (Indigo)   Assemble patio furniture
- (Indigo)   Paint headboards
- (Indigo)   Hang curtain rods
- (Indigo)   Assemble futon
- (Indigo)   Adjust budget
- (Indigo)   Car inspection
- (Indigo)   Set up Quicken
- (Indigo)   Add up receipts
- (Indigo)   Readjust budget

Mrs. Fledaway "laced her husband's tea with atropine in the spring of 1903 at the Locusts, near Puddingbasin, Mortshire" and I wrote things down simply to cross them off my list. "Laundry." "Make bed." My middle son, Ben, had sent an e-mail that read:

"Keep breathing." If only I could have crossed that off! During those days there was nothing to do but keep breathing and mark off the days in the wreckage of time.

Funny how I thought that on this side of it the pain would sub-side and I'd heal. Yet there were mornings I'd wake up after bad dreams and have no will to move, no heart to think about what I'd do if I stepped out of the bed. It surprised me that my heart was still beating at all. I didn't understand why it hadn't given up the way every other part of me had given up. But it pumped on and on, keep-ing its rhythms, keeping things going.

My life and everything in it hadn't stopped aching since I'd started this praying — when was it? — September? October? Anyway, the praying had been unleashed, and now pain was every-where, I can't say why. I needed a night not to feel it. One night, still at my sister's before I'd moved into my new home, I lit the candle but blew it out. I decided I wasn't going to pray. It hurt too much. I needed a night off.

I climbed into bed and was reading a book my son had asked me to read, about Sumerians being from the twelfth planet. The author wasn't a bad writer given the magnitude of information he consoli-dated. But he should have footnoted his sources, and this irked me. I put the book down and picked up my journal instead.

I was nearing the end of it. I'd kept it all that hard year. I'd writ-ten in pencil, thinking the pages would fade over time and the sad narrative be erased. Till then I'd avoided finishing the last pages thinking there'd soon be another story to tell. But the story hadn't changed much. It was still cold. I was still writing checks with no income; still waiting for Bill the Builder — rather, Ernie the tile man — to finish the backsplash.

The pages of that journal had begun before my house had sold; before I had stomach pains; before I got hit by a car from behind; before I had surgery and spent Thanksgiving alone; before I stood before the judge and told him about church; before I loaded a truck (driven by my son Nate) and moved into my sister's basement apartment. I had a few pages left to finish out thoughts about that long year. It had ended horribly, with tears and candles and prostrate praying and gallstones and stomach cramps. I'd said good-bye to my agent in these pages. "I wish you well," he said when we spoke our good-byes. How I missed him, though I doubted he missed me. He e-mailed me once, then wrote a second time because I hadn't responded to the first, despairing of him. He pressed me: "Let me know how you are." So I told him. "I'm debilitated and need you to tell me what to do" (the way he had so many times). He wrote back and said to give myself space, maybe take a trip to Grand Rapids. He thought it would be therapeutic — his point being there are book editors there I could meet with. I wrote that I didn't see going to GR as therapeutic. He asked (writing back) if I was officially divorced, and if so, how I felt. I wrote, "Yes. Sad." We didn't communicate much after that.

I missed my sons, two at college; my oldest living in the north. I longed for them and missed our chats and hikes in the woods and baking cookies for them and hearing their groans of rapture. I plodded on.

I finished the journal: "Ernie the tile man fell and hurt his leg so needs 'a few days off' before he grinds out the wrong-colored grout he put in all the bathrooms." There was so much to be thankful for, I knew. Things like the sound of my sister's family's footsteps over my head. The smell of her soup. Visits (to the basement) from my nieces and nephew who'd chat with me and hear stories about their mom and me at their age. These were God's gifts in an otherwise disorienting world. "I'm thankful, " I wrote, "though I must say I'm glad I've come to the end of this book."

That night, after the journaling, I went to the window and looked at the moon. It rose high and filled the night sky with strange shadows. Clouds circled it, sometimes hiding it, then it would peek through to paint silver and blue over trees. My eyes were wet. Sometimes I looked and saw four moons, then six, even seven, as if it were trying to say, *My beauty cannot be contained in one sphere.*

I relit the candle. I vowed to pray only twenty minutes. I met it, or prayer met me. I did not know the ins and outs of these transactions on my knees by candlelight. I only knew it wouldn't let me go. I had to pray. And if it didn't kill me, I might find my way through the despair to the other side.

<hr/>

My brother-in-law, nephew, and some of his buddies lugged my worldly supplies into my little home in early February. "I like your new place, Aunt Wendy," my dear nephew said. Then he hugged me good-bye.

I was alone. I hung curtain rods and battled the up-and-down finessing of window shades. I assembled the frame of the futon. I carried out the trash. I moved furniture and hung pictures on the walls and put up shelves by myself. Do you know how hard it is to hang a shelf alone? I became adept at drilling holes for plastic screw anchors. I cleaned. I grocery shopped, trying not to buy what I knew my sons would like. Every day I was alone. I tried to come up with a way to receive the day fully, even in my solitude.

I'd have prayers about it. I didn't want to be alone. I wrote bad poetry to calm myself: "You don't have to dismiss these longings, only dethrone them." I moved from day to day between despair and sober judgment.

The Lord God had said, "Divorce is like wearing a blood-stained jacket."[1] So I bought a red blazer at a resale shop and made it the garment of my mourning, my mark. I wore it whenever I went out in public, the way Job donned sackcloth and put ashes on his head. I didn't know what to ask for when I prayed, other than for mercy — that my steps would not be made of myself, for I did not know the way forward. Sometimes, during these prayers, I'd hear God say, *Go where there is light.*

"Let us hide ourselves in the great mountain of his might who dwells concealed in the midst of a forsaken people," Merton wrote.[2] I was reading a lot of Merton in those days, his forte (among other things) being "solitude" issues. He said solitude is a "recollection of God" — a way of gathering him back to a fragmented soul, like mine, who'd lost him or at least had lost a unified picture of who he is. How could I know God when I'd lost a unified picture of who *I* was? I saw only parts — strange parts — that afflicted me and whispered in my ear, *You sorry thing.* It distorted me and I did not love myself. With inner testimonies so distorted, how could I love God? I could not

even love my neighbor. On all fronts, after the divorce, inner sound-
ness was lost to me, and I groped and thrashed, thinking the twisted
parts were all there was.

Merton said the "recollection" of God that comes through solitude is simply the "rediscovery that God remembers us." In my flesh
I cried to be remembered! In my solitude I was given eyes to see that
he who is my portion on earth and my desire in heaven did remember me. He found me. He made the effort. Earthly longings echoed
the desire to see this consolation in flesh and blood. Loneliness in
solitude gave me eyes to see the "invisible companionship" of God.[3]

Our desert was to trample the despair, not to consent to it,
Merton said. "Trample it down under hope in the Cross. Wage war
against despair unceasingly. If we wage it courageously, we will find
Christ at our side."[4]

The few times I'd attended church after leaving my husband's
(once with Caitlin and Ali; once with my sister's family) I ended up
crying. The time had come to find my way back. I knew it was the
only way to trample my despair and restore my inner judgments. I
didn't want to go. At the same time, I had nowhere else to go.

I wore my red blazer. The mountains were cruel that morning.
Snow blew past my window as if to dare me to try and go on. I went
and made my way to a small church in town. The sermon, preached
by an interim pastor, focused upon the "future." She said, "We can
be assured that the future will never be a simple recitation of the
past." When the Jewish exiles who'd been living in Babylon were

given the opportunity to return to their native land of Judah, some hesitated, she said. They'd married outside the tribe of Israel, had built houses and planted fields. The land of their exile had become home. "It is tempting to become like the Hebrews who did not want to leave their homes in Babylon," she said. "But that is not the way of the Lord. God is with us in every changing moment of our lives. God is out there ahead of us, making water in the wilderness."

The service took a surprise turn when she called the children forward, asking them to help in a special celebration. She said to them, and to us in the pew, she thought it was a good idea now and then to rehearse one's baptismal vows. It is necessary sometimes to be reminded of the waters of our baptism and to remember the waters of Jesus' baptism because he didn't ignore hurting people. "Jesus would start to teach, then all of a sudden the roof starts coming apart" — she referred to the friends of the crippled man lowering him through the roof to see Jesus. "There was nothing to do but stop and deal with the situation," she said. "Jesus couldn't ignore the hurting people who gathered around him." In the same way, "God makes water in the wilderness," she said.

The children about her, she prayed from the Prayer Book: "Heavenly Father, we thank you that by water and the Holy Spirit you have bestowed upon these your servants the forgiveness of sin, and have raised them to the new life of grace. Sustain them, O Lord, in your Holy Spirit. Give them an inquiring and discerning heart, the courage to will and to persevere, a spirit to know and to love you, and the gift of joy and wonder in all your works. Amen."[5]

She asked the congregants to rise, then proceeded through the aisles holding the branch of a fir tree, the children following with a bowl of the holy water. She'd turn and dip the branch and wave it over the people, dousing wetness over our heads. People were wiping their glasses. With every sprinkling, she said: "By this water of baptism" . . . and the children echoed: "Remember your baptism."

I did not cry that day. The wetness on my face came by way of a wet branch waved by a joyous priest. She and the children made their way through the sanctuary, then stood before the altar. She prayed: "We thank you, Almighty God, for the gift of water. Over it the Holy Spirit moved in the beginning of creation. Through it you led the children of Israel out of their bondage in Egypt into the land of promise. In it your Son Jesus received the baptism of John and was anointed by the Holy Spirit as the Messiah, the Christ, to lead us, through his death and resurrection, from the bondage of sin into everlasting life.

"Now sanctify this water, we pray you, by the power of your Holy Spirit, that those who here are cleansed from sin and born again may continue forever in the risen life of Jesus Christ our Savior."[6]

Spring

CHAPTER SEVEN

FACE UPSTREAM

⸙

*T*he pace is slower here," the literature said about my new town. "You can enjoy a cup of coffee at one of our cafés, or find that perfect gift for that special person back home. Go biking, hiking, or just sit awhile." I'd moved to the self-described "front porch of western North Carolina," a mountain town, 2,400 feet, nestled in the spur of the Black Mountains along the southern stretch of Blue Ridge. The railroad carved its way through this pass in the late 1800s, and my town was born. The old depot still sits near the town center, an art gallery now, displaying creations of local artists. Brick storefronts with colorful awnings line the three oddly angled streets that converge on the main corner. The "grand old mountains" in rolling ridges as the background for every horizon, town streets are lined with used bookstores, quirky antique shops, music stores with handmade dulcimers, a map store from which my sons bought me a three-dimensional topographical map depicting every mountain peak in the region. Locals gather at the café where you can bring your own mug and sit on worn couches or at tables you shuffle yourself. Benny the barber is known for his command of town news and a decent haircut for under ten bucks. He rarely sweeps his floor.

Many commented upon learning I lived there, "Oh I love your town. I'm sure you must love it too."

I hoped for the day I would love my new town. For all the beauty and mystery of the mountain ranges surrounding me, even after these many months I felt more a ghost than a person. I'd walk daily on the path surrounding the lake near my home, with its unassailable view of the mountain chain called The Seven Sisters, who greeted me, though I didn't always see them. On many days my gaze was low. I'd pass ducks in their troops, and clamoring snow geese, the busybodies of the lake. I'd walk and walk, and the chitchat I'd catch in snatches intensified my feeling of aloneness. A man in a baseball cap in stride with two others was saying in animated gestures "... it just seems strange to me because ..." Three boys on camp stools, tackle boxes at their feet, were casting fish lines when one sneezed: "Aaachooo!" Another said, "Halla." Third one said, "Halla. Halla." I walked passed two young African Americans, the little one imitating a singer with a guitar: "Nee-ow, nee-ow, nee-ow." The older one said, "Quit tryin' to be like no white boy. You already bad." Each step reminded me that for all the ducks in groups and birds in clusters; the fishermen and power-walkers and rock-star wannabes, I trod this path alone. I wish I knew why whatever it was had seemed strange to that man in the baseball cap. How fun to have someone say "Halla Halla" when you sneezed, or to hear the encouragement, "You already bad." I was a life with edges only, an ache I couldn't dispel. One day carried me to the next when whatever came along retrieved me.

Newly settled in western North Carolina's "front porch," my despair in small ways trying to be "trampled" back in church, I decided to explore this new world of rhododendron forests and mountain trails. I was reading Annie Dillard's *Pilgrim at Tinker Creek* at the time, which seemed apropos, being as it is a soliloquy about life, big and small, fierce and splendid, in a mountain wood near Tinker Creek.

As I got into the book, however, I began to wonder how so tedious a monologue about entomological, biological, and infinitesimal living and dying and breeding by and near a creek could possibly have commanded a Pulitzer Prize. How much does one need to know of the life cycles of the dragonfly nymph and the patricidal cannibalistic habits of the ichneumon? Or the "molting frenzies" of the clothes moth that gets smaller every time it molts, until — the size of a molecule — it needs to molt again? Is there not enough bad news?

"The whole creation is one lunatic fringe," Dillard wrote, and I began to perceive a connection to my life. The female praying mantis eats her male sex partner and the giant water bug paralyzes its frog-victim with enzymes that turn its insides to mush and then sucks them out — a metaphor, I thought, for what I felt like. Dillard noted this in shocking detail.

She also said nature asserts itself toward life and that the life-part must be "stalked" over and over. You do that by "facing upstream," she said. "Just simply turn around; have you no will?"[1]

Near my home was a trail called Look Out. Along the path up the mountain, before my ascent, I'd sometimes stop and sit along the creek and try to think about what Annie Dillard might see if she were sitting here with me. I'd bring plastic to sit upon under a bush by the creek, the ground being soaked by spring rains. "There is muscular energy in sunlight," Dillard had written.[2] The way it fell on a moss-covered rotting log, with the combination of shadows and light, made even the rot assert life.

Then I'd hike. It wasn't an easy ascent, but doable in the company of rhododendron and honeysuckle. I'd stop now and then to take in the view of surrounding mountains, valleys, and distant forests draped in green. Every direction I'd look, I could see summits, masses of rock flanked with cuts and escarpments, flowing streams, thickets of laurel, vines and mosses, evergreen woods of balsam. There were no frozen peaks on these mountains. The springs ran cold and clear out of the mountain's heart. The volume of water was astonishing.

I didn't speak my fears on Look Out. I didn't name them or cry them or even pray them. Old earth held the weight of them and kept them in its timeworn heart. Leaves pressed softly beneath my feet. Trees lent roots to pull me upward. Mist settled and the mountains wore clouds like robes. I didn't carry my fears. "You can heave your spirit into a mountain," Dillard had said, "and the mountain will keep it, folded, and not throw it back."[3] Laurels bloomed the universe in pink and green. Leaf upon leaf, stem upon leaves and stems, upon and upon, everything said, *this way; follow it.*

⚓

I wanted to "face upstream" and meet my new life, yet I wasn't sure how. Perhaps I had "no will." I feared the real and present creek would come at me full force, roll and knock me into the creek bed faceup, icy waters spilling over me in surges that would make stiff fingers blue. This fear immobilized me.

This was my "desert" — remembering Merton's words: to trample despair under hope in the Cross. To wage war against it unceasingly, which implied an ongoing effort. This in turn found me trampling it over and over, in my hobbled way, back in the context of church.

By this point, the church had called their new rector, a man named Scott. His first sermon focused on the cleansing of the Temple. As he put it, "Jesus went in and made hay."

The event took place in the court of the Gentiles, an area that had been set apart for nonJewish seekers. It was so "crammed full with animals and money changers," Scott said, the Gentile seekers had been pushed out. They couldn't seek God even if they wanted to, which understandably aroused Jesus' indignation. "Making money to sell the sacrifices for God was a very successful business," he said. The money changers were using others' obedience to the law as a pretext for their greed to the exclusion of those who genuinely sought God, Scott said. "Jesus was overturning more than tables. He was trying to make a point." The hubbub demonstrated the clash of the former things with the new thing Jesus was doing, he said. "Jesus cleansed the Temple of the abuses and arrogance of the powerful, to remove the barriers against what God himself had made freely accessible."

"We ask in times of trouble, *Where is God?*" Then Scott answered his own question: "Wherever there is suffering, God is there."

We had sung a psalm that morning taken from the book of Jonah: "I sank beneath the waves / and death was very near; / The waters closed around me / and seaweed wrapped itself around my head. / I sank down to the very roots of the mountains. / I was locked out of life/ and imprisoned in the land of the dead."[4]

"God comes not in shouts or verbiage, but in simple presence," Scott said. "He gives an invitation to all people to come to the altar and extend their hands to receive the body and blood of Christ, to take the presence of Christ into their hearts."

That day a youth group was visiting from another area. I watched as they sallied to the rail to receive the Eucharist. Wearing blue jeans and lots of black, tattooed, pierced, and long-haired, one after another these young people kneeled and cupped their hands. I saw old men go who could barely hobble on canes; and young men in J. Crew khakis; children in polished shoes; women in back-to-earth wear and others in pressed suits; people with canes; a mentally handi-capped man clutching a little stuffed dog; doctors and college profes-sors and lawyers in tweed — they all went and they all kneeled and raised their cupped hands. Then I went. I felt the waters close around me and seaweed wrapping itself around my head. *What if you're not there?* I lifted my cupped hands. Father Scott pressed a wafer to my palm: "The body of Christ. The bread of heaven." The chalice-bearer followed with the cup: "The blood of Christ. The hope of salvation."

I thought how defenseless Jesus was, his arms stretched wide, tired arms pulled end to end, pinned down with nails, helpless and exposed. In a small way it's what coming to the rail felt like, a laying down of self-defense. I saw in Rome shortly after that, two paintings that cap-tured the feeling brought on at the rail. At the apex of the Church of Santa Maria del Popolo reside two paintings by the late-renaissance painter Caravaggio (1573–1610). They hang face-to-face on opposite walls, one to the left of the altar, the other to the right. The painting on the right, *The Conversion of St. Paul*, shows a strapping young man flat on his back, arms splayed helplessly, face to the sky, eyes closed, and being nearly trampled by his horse. On the left is Caravaggio's *The Martyr of St. Peter*: an old man being nailed upside down on a cross beam, craning his head to look up, eyes wide, old tired arms stretched end to end, bloodied hands pinned down with nails.

The chapel was dimly lit and Caravaggio is known for his experimentation with light. One had to look hard to overcome shadows and bad lighting and capture the force of these works. (My son Ben, who was with me, said, "You can see them better in the postcards.") I noted that in both scenes, one of staggering death, the other of staggering new life, the arms of two strong men were opened wide, incapable of self-defense, leaving them helpless and exposed. It reminded me of words Scott had often uttered from the Prayer Book: "He stretched out his arms upon the cross and offered himself, in obedience to your will, a perfect sacrifice for the whole world." It seems unnatural to stretch one's arms open wide. It is the picture of trust, a relinquishment of self-defense, courageous and odd and bracing, like going to the rail or facing upstream.

One doesn't usually find oneself like that. In fact, one tries very hard not to be found like that. Light broke for Paul on a roadside under his horse with no plea but dirt on his back and arms reaching up. Peter's blush of death found him also strangely aglow, craning his neck hanging upside down. Perhaps the painter wanted to communicate that Peter and Paul beheld the world as it really was, a vision seen clearer with defenses dropped and arms stretched wide. A vision of life facing upstream.

"The body of Christ. The bread of heaven. The body of Christ. The bread of heaven."

I held the wafer in both hands. *Have your way with me.*

Do words carry power?

Have your way.

Do words bring cosmic realignments?

Do what you must.

"This is the blood of Christ, the hope of salvation."

I dipped.

Have your way.

The body and blood felt warm on my lips.

Whatever it takes.

The words ran over and over again through my mind.

<hr>

By the time I finished *The Pilgrim at Tinker Creek,* I understood why Annie Dillard won the Pulitzer Prize. Reading it, I learned that the sun's energy on a square acre of land can produce 4,500 horsepower. That summer conceals what winter reveals. That shadows make sense of the light. ("They inform the eyes of my location.") I learned that we could ignore the 1,356 living creatures in each square foot ("865 mites, 265 springtails, 22 millipedes, and 19 adult beetles"), but doing so won't stop their being there. That if you can't see the forest for the trees, then look at the trees. I learned that 10 percent of all species are parasitic insects and that an Eskimo shaman said,

"Life's greatest danger lies in the fact that men's food consists entirely of souls." That you can wait forgetful anywhere, because "anywhere is the way of his fleet passage"; and that nature's battle loves death more than life. We who live are fellow survivors, "frayed, nibbled, aging, eaten," and who "have done [our] share of eating too."[5]

I learned that something is already here and more is coming.

"Divinity is not playful," Dillard wrote at the end of the book. "The universe was not made in jest but in solemn incomprehensible earnest. By a power that is unfathomably secret, and holy, and fleet. There is nothing to be done about it, but ignore it, or see."[6]

"Remember your baptism," the children had said. When I think of what it felt like to face upstream, to meet the real and present creek, I remember those waters. Sometimes I feared they'd roll over me and my lips would go blue. I'd go to the rail where the uncharted course of God's purpose would meet me, arms stretched wide, helpless and exposed. Sometimes the river ran cold through me. *Let the waters surge. The Lord Almighty is coming here.*[7]

I'd climb Look Out. I'd heave my spirit and it would rest, folded and not thrown back; leaf upon leaf, stem upon leaves and stems, upon and upon like an ever-flowing stream.

One time I sat alone on a rock at the top. The sun fell warm against my face. An old man appeared. He'd mounted the last step to the summit. There we were, only the two of us draped in silence and a tender breeze at the top of the mountain. He turned to head back down. I said, "Don't leave because of me."

He said, "Oh, I'm not. I make the climb just to reach this spot. Making the climb, that's the thing."

Chapter Eight

STRIP YOUR ALTAR

The holy irony for me is that the spiritual death of the Dark Night, "the awful dereliction of the soul closed in upon itself,"[1] as Merton calls it, reached its nadir the weekend of our Lord's passion and resurrection.

On the evening of Maundy Thursday I'd entered the dimly lit sanctuary where two glowing candles adorned the altar. All crosses were shrouded in red linens. The service commenced and Scott prayed, "Mercifully grant that we may receive the sacrament thankfully, in remembrance of Jesus Christ our Lord who in these holy mysteries gives us a pledge."

"Maundy" originated from the Latin *mandautam,* which means "command," he said. Jesus left us a command that night. "That is what Maundy Thursday is about."

We sang:

> He split the hard rocks in the wildness/
> and gave them drink as from the great deep./
> He brought streams out of the cliff/
> and the waters gushed out like rivers./
> But they went on sinning against him,/

rebelling in the desert against the Most High./
They tested God in their hearts,/
demanding food for their craving. (FROM PSALM 78)

Jesus' command signified by Maundy Thursday, Scott said, was embodied in the words, "Take. Eat. Do this in my remembrance."

"Was ever another command so obeyed? Open yourselves to the grace moments in the Eucharist. Receive from my unworthy hands a thin wafer of hope."

That night, sitting in the darkened sanctuary amid shrouded crosses and slow-burning candles, I felt his death close in. He'd asked his friends to stay with him and pray, but they fell asleep. I imagine it was a mercy, so heavy was the night. He went out alone and prayed, nose to the ground, tortured and weeping, snorting like a mule. I tried to picture it: his hands like ropes of the kind they used to pull in trader ships, thick and rough. They were hands that could snap my arm. But the man with ropes for hands I did not fear. He did not snap the arms of women. He'd touched women and allowed women to touch him. One kissed his feet. I pictured him alone in the night, wetness covering him, and howling like a mule. I wanted to kiss him. I looked at his hands thick like the neck of an ox, and I imagined him clutching my quail-bone wrist. I pictured him leading me in slow steps. He'd know my legs were weak. He'd turn to say, *Be careful and watch there*, and point to a patch of ground where the earth collapsed in on itself. My heart would spasm and I'd lose my breath. *I need to stop*, I'd say. He'd turn. *I'll carry you.* I imagined him throwing his cloak over a shoulder smelling like oil and sweat, rough hands under my arms and legs. He'd hoist me and I'd lose my face in his cloak and smell the sweat and oil from the olive groves. I wondered how many others he'd carried this way; where he got the strength. I wondered if they loved him as I loved him. He'd carry me because my bones were weak. My will couldn't follow on its own. I'd kiss that face, sweat pouring out of him. I'd wipe it clean and speak comfort to him so he'd know the *shalom* of human consolation.

I would have touched him in the brush as he lay on the ground. I would have walked to him and put my knees in the dirt and lay my hand on his hair and told him he didn't have to help people any-more. He didn't have to help me. I know exactly how I would have touched him. I felt like I would have died with the Nazarene.

It was the only time he'd hedged. He asked if there might not be another way. He knew there wasn't, but he had to ask. He loosened the knot that tied him up inside. Only a groan could free it. Then he rose to meet his fate.

Did the aching leave him? Did the dread and indecision retreat? They roughed him up. They struck him when he was down. They demeaned and humiliated him. What else could they do to the One who had laid bare their consciences?

He went to the darkness alone. Now he was asking me to follow. He asked me to take his hand and go with him into the darkness because that was the only way through to the other side, to life.

Could my faith-life until then have been a half-life? Maybe all this time I'd hedged — looking for another way, a loophole, a way to finesse it. Could it be I'd never really taken this hand and followed him to die this death? Could it be I'd never really found life?

Scott said, "The *mandautam* of our Savior was to love one another, serve one another, give thanks, share what you have in remembrance of what Jesus has done and continues to do. As death bore down on him that night, Jesus modeled what we should do to follow."

Attendants brought out bowls and poured water into them and lay them on the floor with towels. Scott invited any who were inclined to rise and come to the front and have their feet washed, and to wash another's feet.

Why did the Lord leave such commands? Why did he make it so hard to follow? Who would wash my feet? I'd be embarrassed, waiting in the front pew, looking, wondering if anyone would notice I'd come. Whose feet would I wash? How do you do it?

It was the night of death. How could I *not go?*

I rose and walked forward and sat. Then I saw Anne, an older woman who'd found me during my first visits to that church, then owned me immediately in her heart. She came forward with a ninety-three-year-old man named Sefton, who rang the church bell each Sunday before the service, rain or shine. Anne said, "You sit and wait while I wash Sefton's feet and he washes mine. Then I'll wash yours."

Anne kneeled and lowered Sefton's white bony foot into the water. Sefton put a hand on her shoulder. She poured water over the tops and around the heels and between the toes. She wrapped each foot in a towel, one at a time, and worked it dry.

Then Sefton kneeled. He needed help getting down. Anne sat in the pew while he washed her feet. Then he sat near me and waited while Anne kneeled a second time, lifting my feet to the water, hands pouring wetness over and under and between the toes. She dried them one at a time.

I stood to return to my pew and saw a dainty woman in a yellow spring dress sitting and waiting alone, probably wondering as I'd wondered, who would wash her feet. I kneeled by her and took the basin and lifted her feet into the water. They were delicate feet, pointy, like a ballerina's. I poured water the way Anne had done with mine, and dried them one at a time. We stood. I embraced her. She said, "What should I do now?"

"You can sit down," I said. "My feet have already been washed."

The woman behind me, who was mentally handicapped, said to the friend sitting next to her, "I felt the Lord come to me. My feet got real warm."

Scott read from the Prayer Book: "The Lord Jesus, after he had supped with his disciples and had washed their feet, said to them, 'Do you know what I, your Lord and Master, have done to you? I have given you an example, that you should do as I have done.'"

The people responded, "Peace is my last gift to you, my own peace I now leave with you; peace which the world cannot give, I give you."

We sang. *Were you there when they crucified my Lord?*

I didn't join in at first. I heard myself say, "No, I wasn't there." What did it look like? What did it sound like? What did it smell like?

I imagined the smell of lentils and wine, of cinnamon and fire and sweat and dirty feet. I pictured wetness in people's eyes, though I imagined the seeing wasn't as bad as the smelling or the hearing. I imagined voices, the clatter of stones. "Ha!" Weeping and spitting and rattling sounds. The beating of a stick. A hiccup. A whisper. "Ha!" A groan. *Eloi, Eloi.*

I felt inside myself the strangeness of that day, like my joints moved backward, like I walked on broken legs.

I pictured a hill and a sign, white on black. There was a hyssop branch and a purple robe and a sponge and a flinty spear — accoutrements that went with the display. I imagined the hillside smelling of pottage and smoke and burning fat and the sweetness of myrrh. And bodily smells, sweat, waste, blood, the blending of the foul with the sweet. Seeing, I imagine, wasn't the point.

Were you there when they laid him in the tomb?

"I wasn't," I heard myself say. "But I'm here now. I'm thinking about it."

My God, my God! Why have you forsaken me?
Why do you remain so distant?
Why do you ignore my cries for help?
Every day I call to you, my God, but you do not answer.
Every night you hear my voice, but I find no relief.
My life is poured out like water,
and all my bones are out of joint.
My heart is like wax,
melting within me.
My strength has dried up like sunbaked clay.
My tongue sticks to the roof of my mouth.
You have laid me in the dust and left me for dead.
My enemies surround me like a pack of dogs;

an evil gang closes in on me.
They have pierced my hands and feet.
I can count every bone in my body.
My enemies stare at me and gloat.
They divide my clothes among themselves
and throw dice for my garments.[2]

In the silence of that dark sanctuary, after the service had ended, people started stripping the altar. The candles went out and were carried off. The palm branches, red shrouds over crosses, the red altar covering — all were taken away, as were the crosses themselves, save one. It stood alone on the table, the red cloth replaced with black. Everything was gone except that one black-shrouded cross. The silence, the emptiness, the darkness, the heaviness of all the sadness in the world closed in.

Where am I? What was my greatest fear? I heard myself say, Lay it down in the darkness where he laid down his fear. My deepest, most intimate, tortured, unresolved heartbeat must go into the darkness and die where he died. The nails went through his wrists and life was wrung out of his beating heart. His aching had been long gone. My aching made me ready to receive this death. I had to feel it as he felt it, defenseless, vulnerable. Lay it down. Put it where he died. Take it to his death.

Is this where my madness has led me? To your death? Only the mad can see it.

Take my hand.

I'll follow you. Only take my hand.

May your blessings rest on your people.

The grave wraps ropes around me.

You open heaven.

Dark storm clouds are beneath your feet.

You shroud yourself in darkness.[3]

CHAPTER NINE

RECEIVE YOUR NEW GARMENTS

❦

*F*or the next two days I did not speak to anyone. I was in silence and alone, Black Friday and Saturday. At times I feared what would become of me, being so alone. Tears would rise to my eyes. The weight of it covered me like seventy-five pounds of aloes and myrrh that covered him who carried my heart with him to the grave. Then I'd think, *Who in this life doesn't suffer? Who doesn't fight to claw through another day?* The grave wasn't empty yet.

I'd chosen not to go to the Good Friday service, weary as I was of death themes. I rented a movie instead. It was called *Signs* and starred Mel Gibson, who always cheered me up. It examined the faith struggle of a priest who'd abandoned his calling after the untimely death of his wife. It involved crop circles and the invasion of aliens. The ex-priest — Mel Gibson — lived on a farm with his two young children and his younger brother, played by Joaquin Phoenix. One day the children started sensing the presence of something weird, aliens it turned out, and crop circles appeared in the corn fields. Aliens had arrived. The terror they evoked reduced Mel Gibson back to a praying man. Only with God's help could he and his family (and the world) be saved. The aliens retreated.

I hadn't ached that day. I imagined myself being led into the darkness, Jesus holding my hand the way Mel Gibson took his little girl's when the aliens threatened to harvest her soul. Jesus went before me, holding my hand, and Mel Gibson went before his little girl. Sometimes my heart spasmed and I couldn't breathe. Sometimes my soul buckled in on itself. Then he carried me. I could smell his breath.

The movie felt contrived. I felt no terror watching it. I felt like my heart had left me. I imagined aliens arriving, my soul buckling in on itself, and the worst — *the worst* — that could happen was that I'd die alone. Aliens would come with their crop circles and shadow people's doorways and hide in people's pantries, the way they hid in Mel Gibson's pantry. They would terrorize towns and nations and CNN would cover it. People would be harvested — empty shells of human remains *left behind* à la Jerry Jenkins (get it?). I'd be alone in my home when the end of the world would come. I'd be in my soft green bowl chair, the one I bought at Pier 1 for $79. I'd die alone and wouldn't fear aliens because a woman with nothing to lose has no fear and, who knows? I may never be found because the world would be ending everywhere and people might not think to call. I'd die in my home with "0" on my message machine. When the world would end, I'd be alone in my house and the moment of death would end all fears and I wouldn't remember the feeling of dying alone, nor would I have to keep thinking about living alone because I would have already faced the Worst Case Scenario. Thinking of it (for once) didn't make me cry.

Then, Sunday morning at 12:37 AM I passed from death to life. Hopelessness awoke to possibility.

How it came to be that hope — or a kind of hope — returned to me Easter morning at 12:37 AM, I cannot explain. The moment was shocking, subtle, disarming, and out of the blue all at the same time. I was having toast and milk in my kitchen to beat back insomnia. I put my dishes in the sink, turned the corner, and was walking around the bar stool to my right, shuffling my cold feet across the wood floor toward the stairway. Then something lifted. The thought came, *Maybe the suffering will end. Maybe, even, happiness will come. Why exclude it as a possibility?*

For, you see, the most wretched, helpless, and terrifying aspect of the journey into the Dark Night is the weight of it and the feeling it will never end. That is why the moment something lifted, whatever it was, so shocked me. I did not swoon. My head did not spin. But relief came. It was as simple as that. I felt the onus had been lifted off me, and that even *my life* was not beyond the reach of joy.

This was the point of the journey, to return to G. K. Chesterton's metaphor, where the descent reached its nadir and I stepped across the invisible line that transferred the process to an upward incline.

Hope of a kind returned to me at 12:37 AM and nudged me into believing *it could be* that God himself has dreams for me. *It could be* that the ache of loss, disorientation, and even hopelessness I was carrying these many months was God himself praying through it to effect his will, *his* deepest longings. Maybe it was his ache. Who knows? Why count it out?

The moment seemed to say, *Life will come back to you. You will live.* I would have welcomed further clarification — terms, you know. But it was sufficient to have been given that much: You have been dead and now you will live. Life will return to you.

I didn't know what it meant by "life" and I didn't know when or how the returning to it would unfold for me. I thought I might issue a request. Then I thought, the less I have to say about how life returns to me, probably the better off everyone would be.

⁂

The worship service Easter morning opened with trumpets. The woman whose feet I'd washed wore dainty silver slippers. The other woman, the one whose feet had felt warm, sat next to me. She wore purple velour and kindly pointed out to me the page number for the opening hymn. Her hands trembled when she sang. She rocked left and right. During the doxology she raised her palms, arms bent at the elbows, and bowed her head at the part that says, "Praise Father, Son, and Holy Ghost."

I was remembering a dream I'd had. It had to do with a funeral taking place in what looked like an old but refined luxury hotel with bellhops and brass elevators. In the "lobby" I saw a coffin high on a bier, the lid open and the corpse wrapped in cloth, like a mummy. People came over and started to lift the coffin and carry it to the sanctuary for the funeral. I remember feeling sad, seeing the body wrapped like that, being lifted and carried for the funeral.

I was looking at the mummy and saw something move. Then it moved again and turned and twisted. Soon I saw hair, brownish-auburn, and then a round ruddy face of a woman. She wore her hair short with curls. She had been dead, wrapped in linens and in fact was being carried in to her own funeral when life returned and she moved her head and wriggled free from the linens that had enshrouded her. Her face was neither anguished, nor sublime. Maybe a little confused.

Scott was saying in his sermon that Sunday morning, "Something very dramatic, beyond explanation, occurred that first Easter that influenced the course of the world. All of us have had our own crucifixion times when we were backed into a corner with nowhere to turn and no hope for tomorrow. It is called the dark night of the soul, when we are holding on to — or being held up by — a thin thread of grace.

"God's grace working through the sacrament of the body and blood is the greatest hope we can hold on to. It's here and it's there. It's visible and it's invisible. It fills all creation with hope."

The woman in purple velour kneeled beside me in the pew. She rocked front and back, putting her hand on her heart when we sang, *Alleluia. Christ our Passover is sacrificed for us. Therefore let us keep the feast. Alleluia.*

I went to the rail to receive the body and the blood of Christ, and Father Scott pressed a wafer in my cupped hands. The body of Christ, the bread of heaven. Anne was the chalice-bearer that day. She smiled as she lowered the chalice. "Wendy, this is the blood of Christ, the hope of salvation." I held back my tears. Returning to the pew I kneeled. *O God, let your light reach my darkest place. Let your mercies come. Let them rise with your holy purpose.*

The woman whose feet I'd washed left the service with wet eyes, as I did. We'd sung a hymn of praise to the power of the Father, Son, and Holy Spirit and, singing it, I knew that it was so — really knowing it for the first time in many years. A kind of hope had returned to me at 12:37 AM and I could not say a hope for what. I knew only that in this life there was a time to die and a time to live, and I sensed, by the mercies of God and by the clock that signaled 12:37, that the journey had changed course and that I would not die, but live. Augustine called the process, "laboring under the pain of the new life that was taking birth."[1] This day, when heaven and earth together rose and the morning star brightly shone, the Red Sea opened and the people were delivered from their gloom. They walked on dry land. The woman in my dream wearing death linens turned her head. Her cheeks were red. Her hair hadn't lost its curls. She awoke from death, bewildered but alive.

A few Sundays later, the morning of the "Dedication of the New Altar Hangings," Scott preached about the time Jesus returned to visit Nazareth. "What could be more secure than being in his hometown church?" he said. "Before he was finished preaching they were ready to throw him off a cliff — what were those folks there in Nazareth thinking about?"

Scott said, "Rejection and acceptance are the themes of every life. We need to have courage to persevere."

He told a story of a nurse who once was asked, "In all your years, what has been the most courageous thing you saw?" The nurse answered, "It was a five-year-old boy with a dying sister." Only he, the little boy, had the antibodies to cure her disease, the nurse said. When he settled himself on the table to prepare for the transfusion, he looked up at the nurse and asked, "When I start to die will it hurt?"

"Faith-filled courage makes a meaningful life," Scott said. "A friend from seminary told me once, 'They may kill you out there, but we will never be defeated.' The last best highest devotion will not be in vain. The world will know God's servants have been among them."

The time had come for the dedication of the new altar hangings. It was a lovely quilted mountain landscape, glistening linens of greens, blues, silver, and gold. The sky was festooned with golden-winged creatures, birds or angels (if there's a difference), little Holy Spirits everywhere. Tall brass candlesticks commanded the edges of the table where two vases of white and red roses with daisies splayed heavenward mixed with fronds of green, the cross rising between.

Scott prayed, "This offering which you shall receive from the people — gold, silver, bronze, blue and purple and scarlet cloth, and finely woven linen. O Lord my God, how excellent is your greatness. You are clothed with majesty and splendor."

Anne preceded me to the rail for the Eucharist. We kneeled together at the altar with its new garments shining, cupping our hands, lifting them to break through eternity's veil. Anne received it smiling. She turned to me, her eyes shining. I had no prayers left to pray. No deaths left to die. No prayers, no deaths, only trust. The last best highest devotion came by the low road, along the hard way. "O God, may it please you to comfort and relieve those distressed in mind, body, or estate; give them patience under their sufferings and a happy issue out of all their afflictions.[2] May their last best highest devotion not be in vain. Let your mercies come, Good Father, clothed in splendor, gold, silver, bronze, blue and purple and scarlet cloth, a finely woven linen."

I returned to my pew. "You have taken away my clothes of mourning and clothed me with joy."[3] My bloodstained jacket had been removed, replaced with finely woven garments.

Summer

CHAPTER TEN

HOLD ON! HOLD ON!

⟨━━━⟩

*T*he good news was, I'd reached the nadir, taken that hand, turned the corner, and started the ascent. The bad news was, I had as far to go up as I'd already come down and the climb required more grit. It meant pulling dead weight.

By this point I was ready to live. The problem was, I had no strength left with which to undertake life. Falling into the hole as I did at the beginning of this journey, I'd surrendered the terms of rescue; grabbed what ballast I could from everyday miracles; entered the chaos; looked for signs; prayed low; risen, if only a little, to trample despair. I'd turned and faced upstream. I'd taken that hand that stripped off my garments — died that death; then I'd received the chance to be reclothed. I'd turned the corner and thought I'd seen light.

So began the clawing.

The thought possessed me at about this point that perhaps I ought to become a nun. (Did I mention flourishes of insanity attend this journey?) My thinking was, I didn't have my family anymore; my sons had grown and had assumed their own lives. And what does one do with sexuality after more than two decades of marriage? Embrace it? The better option seemed to renounce all I'd been and take up a holy life under the vows of poverty, chastity, and obedience. I thought I might join the Second Order of St. Francis, the Poor Clares. I would be traveling to Italy in the upcoming fall and had a mind to look into it.

It didn't take long to conclude, however, I was not cut from the cloth of St. Clare. I'd pushed three boys through my loins and there was no turning back from that. And I couldn't abide the thought of grandchildren calling me "sister-grandmother." Given the isolation of my new circumstances and the realization I would never be a nun, I concluded instead to "marry my vocation." I would sell my life dearly to what I did best: journalism. I'd go any place and step into any situation and find people who suffered and tell their stories. I would stand in solidarity with them. Maybe I'd die. But why not? How better to die than doing what I did best, and helping hurting people at the same time?

I assaulted my role. That summer, within a single six-week period, I drove to Nashville; St. Louis; Wheaton, Illinois; Grand Rapids, Michigan; down to Springfield and Branson, Missouri; then back to North Carolina only to pack up a few days later for Washington D.C. I squeezed in a drive to Memphis, Tennessee, and Chagrin Falls, Ohio, as well as a trip to Wenham, Massachusetts, before packing my bags for Central America.

I had been given the assignment to go meet the poorest of the poor in Nicaragua. I'd lived in Central America from 1990 to 1994, in Honduras, a country closely linked to Nicaragua's history. But I'd never crossed the border they share. My earliest impression of Nicaragua had come over the evening news the summer of 1979, when, with a random glance at the television I saw a man on his knees and another man in boots and military fatigues standing over him with a gun. Before I knew what I was looking at, the uniformed man raised the gun and aimed its muzzle at the head of the kneeling man, who lurched and fell dead, right there on the evening news. The name associated with the killing had been "Somoza," then dictator of Nicaragua. The event I witnessed on television became the catalyst that sparked one of history's stunning revolutions (more on that later). Anyway, the years I'd lived in Honduras I traveled west, to El Salvador and Guatemala, but never east to the unwelcoming country where helpless men get shot in the head.

In Miami I planned to meet my son Jon, who would accompany me to Managua. The plane approached the Miami airport and I looked out my window at sapphirine skies and wisping clouds. I could see the shadow of our plane floating over the backdrop of a cloud. Then, in a split second, a rainbow appeared encircling the plane's shadow. I had seen many rainbows in my lifetime: arches and double rainbows with colors so astounding you could almost see the edges between the ROY G. BIV. But I had never seen a rainbow like the one out my window approaching Miami. It was a complete circle, the shadow of our plane dead center. For a split second it felt as if my seat in that plane, against the backdrop of blue sky and encircled by a rainbow, was at the bull's-eye of a promise. Then it was gone.

I spent most of the next several days tied at the hip to my translator, Marcos Rodriguez, a dead ringer for Billy Crystal. Marcos, thirty-seven, was a kind and humorous man, a husband and father of two, and former Sandinista border guard who'd fought the guerrilla war against the contras for four years in Nicaragua's northern mountains. In his short lifetime, the brutality of Somoza shaped Marcos's boyhood; and four years of his young adult life were stolen by the communist Sandinistas who conscripted the country's young people to fight their war in mountain jungles. Marcos was conscripted twice (they'd lost his papers after his first tour). From the age of 18 to 22 he slogged through jungles with an AK rifle on his back, wearing soggy boots, sleeping in trees, watching friends and brothers die.

On long drives over rough roads, Marcos and I talked about that. He remembered as a young boy how Somoza's special police force came to his neighborhood and massacred an assembly of young people in a church. "The people didn't have weapons," Marcos said. "We hid in our houses. You could hear everything." In those days almost daily "four or five or six or ten young people were killed. I saw it as a young man. It was a horrible situation."

The people of Nicaragua, he said, "were developing the feeling of rejection toward Somoza. The Sandinistas got organized to fight and overthrow the dictatorship that was oppressing and killing the people." Anyone sympathizing with the Sandinistas — which would have been just about everybody — Somoza hunted down, or tried to.

"Most of the people in Nicaragua, both in the cities and the countryside, got organized and said, 'We're going to overthrow Somoza,'" Marcos said. Their dream came true July 19, 1979, which marked the day of the victory of the revolution. The new Sandinista leadership was little more than a ragtag assemblage of stout-hearted patriots. But they claimed a stunning victory over the entrenched, defiant, ruthless Somoza. The new government failed to understand, however, that people backed their revolution, not as much as a commitment to communism so much as a hope for better days. The poor soon realized ideology didn't feed starving families. But the Sandinistas were ideologues. They found themselves employing the same terror tactics Somoza had used to squelch the revolution, in their own effort to prop it up.

In the early 1980s, the United States set up military camps along the Honduras-Nicaragua border to train and equip counter-revolutionary Nicaraguans, called *contras,* to fight Sandinistas and stop encroaching communism. The Sandinistas responded by forcing Nicaraguan youths to fight the war, young men like Marcos. "The people didn't like that," he said. "Years were passing by and more people were getting killed in the mountains. There was a food shortage because of the U.S. embargo. There was a war. The people did not know what to do. The people were in despair. They developed hatred toward the Sandinistas."

The Somoza regime, the reign of a father and two sons, lasted forty years (1937–1979). The skirmishes that finally overthrew him had gone on for decades. The subsequent civil war against the contras lasted approximately nine years, beginning in 1981, ending in 1990 when Nicaragua held their first free elections.

Nearly everyone I met on that trip had a story shadowed by terror associated with recent history. When we'd speak of it, I saw throats constrict and eyes focus downward. Voices went low, and silences descended. Grief lay just under the surface of these people's otherwise congenial comportment.

I met and interviewed too many Nicaraguans to mention here. But four stood out, all women, each in her own way showing me a small glimpse of myself. In a way, these women helped piece together shards of my own broken story.

The first was named Aleyda, who lived in a neighborhood outside Managua that had been terrorized by Somoza. To get there we took roads of a kind that had Marcos turning from the front seat, head bobbing, to say, "Hold on! Hold on!" (He called our vehicle a *caballo* — a horse.) We mounted a grassy slope to the concrete-block schoolhouse where we were to meet Aleyda. Approaching it, our guide waved a hand and spoke in a low voice, "Dead bodies of many people are buried over here."

Aleyda was a striking diminutive woman with angular cheeks and warm eyes that possessed at the same time an endearing ferocity. She met us outside. With her stood a shriveled crooked man. "His name is Antonio Vargo," she said. "He is very poor. He is not my friend. He is not my relative. But I want to help him in the name of God."

She recounted how she'd grown up in a time when Somoza's guards knocked on doors and pulled villagers from their homes, accusing them of sympathizing with the Sandinistas. She'd witnessed hands being cut off with machetes, neighbors being killed, and knew others who'd "disappeared."

"In those years of war we had many guests in the house. We were helping feed them and hide them because some men were trying to kill them. I saw four or five people dead on the ground. The truth is, I don't like to talk about it because I always feel sad. It was a hard time to be living. I don't want to live it again. The words don't come easily."

Not far away on a dusty patch of ground stood a hovel made from a random assemblage of wood slats and tin. There we met Maritza, twenty-nine, mother of six children she'd borne to a man who was not her husband. We smelled beans cooking over an open fire. Maritza wore a crisp white blouse and held a child on her lap as we talked. Her visage was stoic but tender, with sad eyes and minimal expression. "We are very poor," she said. "Sometimes we are able to provide only one meal a day for our children. Right now I am boiling beans. We ate one time today in the morning. We will eat again in the evening. Just beans, no tortillas." She said she hunted for armadillos when there were no beans. "I feel bad about killing the armadillo. But given the necessity, I have to.

"My parents abandoned me when I was a few days old, so I did not have a birth certificate. Without a birth certificate I was never baptized. An old man adopted me. He gave me his last name, but I was not baptized. I belong to the Catholic church," she said. "Because I am not baptized I cannot be married in the Catholic church. Because we are not married, I cannot take the sacrament. I have felt as if I was an animal, not a person. I have felt as though I didn't exist, that I am nothing.

"Sometimes when I feel I am nothing and nobody is watching me, then I see the hand trying to reach me. God sends someone to each of us to give us hope in life. Then I see the hand that is trying to reach me."

Later that day we traveled to a village high on a ridge along the Pan-American Highway south of Managua. Many wealthy Nicaraguans have built sprawling whitewashed homes on this ridgeline. Amid private schools and coffee farms and beyond the whitewashed haciendas shaded by cedars, lies another neighborhood. This one was marked by mud-thatched homes, outhouses, and bamboo fencing, the home of Juana, age ten. She stood poised and erect as we chatted about her doll, Ana, her favorite toy. "My doll Ana is very pretty. Ana is my little girl. I kiss her and hug her. She wears little skirts and blouses. I change her clothes when she goes to parties." Juana pushed hair from her face. "There are lots of people at the parties. They are dancing.

"I am hoping for another doll to be the friend to Ana. I will name him Juan, Ana's boyfriend. Juan is a tall guy and handsome. He will be kind. He will take care of me and help me. I do not have fears, only dreams," she said.

The farthest reaches of our travels took Jon, Marcos, and me 120 miles north of Managua to the mountain community of San Ramon, near the city center of Matagalpa, a one-time Sandinista stronghold. Fierce battles against the contras took place in this region. Bullet holes were still visible in the stucco siding of some buildings.

The splendor of the mountains — the beauty of palms and acacias, hibiscus and the flamboyan — belied the desperate conditions of the inhabitants of San Ramon, who suffered in the extreme. Being so far removed from Managua, and having been so hard hit from the civil war, the majority of its 16,000 residents did not have access to safe drinking water and other basic services and supplies. Children died regularly because of malnutrition. Most people couldn't read or write.

Our escort for the day was a feisty, intelligent woman named Marilu, thirty-eight. A teacher of Spanish, scholar and poet, she grew up during the war and rose above its tragedies through spirit and sheer grit. She attended university on Saturdays and took a degree in education. "I was nineteen during the [contra] war. It was a chilling situation. In my town the contras were fighting the Sandinistas and unfortunately, I saw many, many people killed. I was traumatized by that. The shooting was all over the town. The contras took their bodies back with them, but the Sandinista bodies were scattered all over. Sometimes the contras would come into town and if they didn't like you they would say, 'You are a Sandinista' or 'You are a friend of the Sandinistas,' and then you die. Of course I was afraid. That psychologically affects you."

She said, "I am a pure Nicaraguan *pinolero* [a typical drink made out of corn]. When people ask me where I am from I tell them: 'I come from a place where the wind comes late; where nobody is best or worst; I come from a place where everybody is equal.' In the world there is no other nation as brave as my nation."

At the day's end, when we said our good-byes, Marilu turned to me and said, "Journalists have something of being a poet in them. The words they write have to be beautiful."

⁂

Our last stop took us to a grassy plain under the shadow of Volcan Momotombo. A community had gathered from surrounding neighborhoods to dedicate the land, the site of a new housing project. We stood with the people in a circle, hats lifted and heads lowered to pray. Trees rustled in the breeze. Children dashed about grabbing balloons and throwing sticks. Momotombo caught the sun's late rays, which painted it in burnished purples and orange. Someone prayed, *Thank you for husbands and families.*

Quiet stirrings arose within me hearing the words "husbands and families." Standing at the base of a mountain where children played and families gathered in hope for new beginnings, I wondered if journalists who tell these stories are beyond the reach of miracles.

I did not have a husband. My kitchen table no longer pulled "my family" to its center. My life was beyond the reach of miracles, I thought. But I had married my vocation. My job was to recount other people's miracles. I stood with the community who would soon build upon that land. They were hopeful. Our heads were low as people prayed and four faces would not depart from me. I saw Aleyda take the arm of that crooked little man who was not her friend and not her relative, but whom she wanted to help in the name of God. For he needed help. She put past losses and nightmares away and risked neighbor love. There was nothing else to do. The world is cruel and damages people. I remembered the eyes of Maritza who thought she didn't exist, or was at best an animal, because she didn't have a birth certificate. Her deepest wish, more than marriage, even existence itself, was to take the sacrament, to worship God. Juana's dreams hadn't died in the ravages of loss. A little girl of ten stood erect and made dreams seem sensible. Marilu told people she came from a place where the wind comes late and nobody is the best or worst, the bravest nation in the world. She said journalists have something of a poet in them.

God is "singing his song in the hearts of the poor," I'd read in a prayer book one time. God's song arose from these heroic women and it made me believe there was a song in me too. I'd have to risk neighbor love and inclinations to worship when I felt more like an animal, and the sensibility of hope and poetic grit. The song I heard in these voices helped me imagine God's song in me, that it would find a way out no matter which way life slayed us.

It takes so little to bring someone hope. I am a journalist who came to tell stories of the poor, and they ended up showing me my story. They lent hands on the first timid steps of the upward climb, like a prayer catching the sun's late rays at the base of a burnished mountain. In every life God sings a song. Husbands and families belong to each other. And in lives where there are no husbands and families, I heard another voice telling me — *Hold on, hold on.*

CHAPTER ELEVEN

FIGHT FOR AIR

One of the more perplexing aspects of the final tortured stages of the Dark Night had been the epiphanies that would come, the steps forward, only to be met on other days with slippages back. I think of Jacob. The eve before he was to meet his brother Esau, whom years before he had betrayed by stealing his father's blessing, he found himself entangled in a match of grit and strength with an unknown being, "a man," whom Jacob later recognized as God himself. Jacob struggled with God *mano a mano* (hand to hand), and prevailed, but not without a wounding. At the break of dawn, after battling through the night, the "man" finally told Jacob to release him. Jacob demanded a blessing, which he received — a new name. He also got his hip wrenched out of the socket. For the rest of his days he walked with a limp. Frederick Buechner, in his novel *Son of Laughter* — a fictional account of the life of Jacob — describes the episode:

> I remember as blessing the one glimpse I had of his face. It was more terrible than the face of dark, or of pain, or of terror. It was the face of light. No words can tell it. Silence cannot tell it. Sometimes I cannot believe that I saw it and lived but that I only

dreamed I saw it. Sometimes I believe I saw it and
that I only dream I live. . . . From that day to this I
have moved through the world like a cripple with the
new name the Fear gave me that night by the river
when he gave me his blessing and crippled me.[1]

I found, oddly, in the last gasps of my struggle a similar odd jux-
taposition. On the one hand, by the late stages of this journey, so
much had been stripped away, and I'd been reduced to naked
dependence and God showed himself tender toward me. On the
other hand, when the battles returned, as inevitably they did, they
became more acute and disabling. Both the blessing and the wounding marked the final groping steps of this journey.

<hr/>

The blessing came through a back door. I'd caught a cold on the plane
and couldn't rise from my bed the morning after my return from
Nicaragua. A few days later I learned I had pneumonia. The first
round of antibiotics did not work. Within two days of completing
them, I was back in bed, feeling worse than before. I began to think
about Jim Henson, creator of the Muppets, who died in 1990 from
"galloping" pneumonia at fifty-three. He thought he had a cold.

"Health is a long and regular work," wrote John Donne, whom
I was reading, which might not have been the best idea since he
seemed preoccupied with death themes. "But in a minute a cannon
batters all, overthrows all, demolishes all; a sickness unprevented for
all our diligence, unsuspected for all our curiosity; nay underserved, . . .

summons us, seizes us, possesses us, destroys us in an instant."[2]

I began the second round of "super" antibiotics and felt no improvement for days. I pictured the obituary: "Death by pneumonia at forty-seven. She was strong until then." I thought I should draw up a will. But I had no lawyer, only software, and possessed no strength to rise from my bed. Maybe I could scribble out a will by hand, I thought. When one is confined to one's bed with fears of galloping pneumonia, living alone in a new town, unable even to go downstairs to fix a bowl of soup, thoughts like these arise.

I had been a woman with nothing to lose, and so nothing to fear. I'd undertaken to sell my life dearly to my vocation. I'd exhausted myself that summer, traveling about, interviewing like a madwoman, culminating in the trip to Nicaragua from which I had not recovered. My well-intended, but alas misguided, plan had backfired.

It wasn't the trip from which I had not recovered as much as from the assault of my actions. I had sold my life, but quickly learned it hadn't been mine to sell. It didn't take long to figure out that I was unable to heal myself, and I was unsure whether the medicines would heal me either. My life, in other words, was not in my hands. I had no control over anything: my recovery; pending contracts; strength and time to write; my finances or dreams (such as they were). I could not plot out my next day's goals. My color-coded day planner had long been put aside. I'd stopped thinking about "doing things."

Sometimes I'd hear a singing bird or a crow squawking. Sometimes there would be a quiet rain or the sound of branches cracking in a tree. Now and then I'd catch sight of a hummingbird outside my window.

I couldn't listen to music because the sound hurt my ears and aroused emotions I didn't have the strength to entertain. I could only lie in my bed under the gentle rotation of my ceiling fan, take my temperature now and then, and think about who I wanted to see before I died.

About the third week of this monotony, the thought occurred to me that the unremitting ache I'd carried these many months had gone away during this illness. Then I realized that the pneumonia *was* the ache — the emotional turned physiological, as if my spirit gave way and my body revolted saying, "Enough. We can carry this no longer. Now it will carry us." My ache had defaulted to physical capitulation. I began to understand I had to put a boundary around my grief so that my lungs could have the chance to heal.

Albert Camus, in his classic work, *The Plague,* described a little town caught off guard with an outbreak of the bubonic plague. He described the town as "treeless, glamourless, soulless and . . . seemingly restful." The blight of the plague, of course, changed everything. "Our townsfolk were not more to blame than others;" he wrote, "they forgot to be modest, that was all, and thought everything still was possible for them; which presupposed that pestilences were impossible."[3]

I hadn't taken health for granted: I understood the gift. I recalled many times on my walks thanking God for legs that could mount this hill and lungs that served to give me breath. At the same time, during my illness, a man I knew who'd been battling cancer, had also contracted lung congestion that killed him within a week. He died of complications with his lungs. Life could be over before we knew what hit us. I couldn't presume health would win over this.

I'd sleep ten hours at night and wake up feeling exhausted. One day would be worse than the previous one. My eyes hurt and head ached and my sinuses were congested and I had no strength. After a month of this, people expected better news, news that I was "feeling better." But I wasn't. I was still in bed. One day was often worse than the day before.

Sometimes terror left my limbs and joints and muscles quaking. I feared the powerlessness of it. I feared the love for life that was awakening inside me. I feared the hope that was arising — I feared losing it, the betrayal of hope. I feared that I had come this far for nothing. That I was climbing out of the hole, only to die in my bed of pneumonia. I'd convulse, wanting to live, to have life back. No! No! I'd hear myself cry. Give me more time!

Despair was once again beating at my door. Its rankness tried to wrestle me and overtake my hope in God.

A preacher I'd heard once said marathon runners didn't run for the exercise; they run for the rhythm. Never having run a marathon, I could not say whether it was so. But the preacher said that just as there is the rhythm of one's pulse; the rhythm of sleeping and waking; the rhythm of our breathing, "there is a rhythm to the revelation of God," the breath of God, he called it. And when runners reach the limits of physical capability, they have to dig deep to find that higher rhythm.

I had reached the limits of my physical capabilities. I needed the higher rhythm, the breath of God to fill my aching lungs. I fought for air. I believed in the rhythms of prayer. I'd pray aloud, "Sanctify, this sickness, O Lord. May I make room for your power to possess me."[4]

I kept "the hours," prayers and psalms read from a manual in the morning, midday, and evening. In the morning I'd pray, "I do not know what this day will bring, O Lord, but make me ready. If I am to stand, help me stand bravely. If I am to sit still, help me sit quietly. If I am to lie low, help me do it patiently. Make these words more than words, and give me the Spirit of Jesus."[5] In the evening I'd light my candle and pray from my bed, "Look down, O Lord, and illumine this night; drive far from it all snares of the enemy; let your angels dwell with me to preserve me in peace."[6]

"How should the [townsfolk] have given a thought to anything like plague," wrote Camus, "which rules out any future, cancels journeys, silences the exchange of views. They fancied themselves free, and no one will ever be free so long as there are pestilences." My hope, until this time, had rested on passing identities — as a mother, the wife of the pastor, a journalist. When I lost my sons to "the empty nest" and also lost my marriage — two of my three identities in one devastating season — in my heart (inasmuch as I could perceive what was in my heart) I fancied I had nothing left to lose and therefore thought myself free to take journeys with nothing to fear. But one is not free as long as there are pestilences. My sickness took the last of my temporal identities — my vocation. I'd sold myself dearly and God gave me my way. I realized it now. I understood life itself, not its passing identities, was God's sacred mysterious gift. I'd thought I had nothing to fear. Yet now I confronted a different kind of fear. I'd found, after all, I did have something to lose: life itself, a chance for God to sing his song in me; a second chance to put my hope in him.

Hope had returned, but this time not from ill-conceived con-cocted versions of changing identities. The dying process I'd under-gone inside myself had forged new borders. Or better, new borders had been drawn about me, formed by God's smelting furnace and not from life's passing phases. How could I have thought that my sorry life of all sorry lives in this wearisome world was so spectacu-lar as to be the one to get left behind? Camus had said that "the habit of despair is worse than despair itself."[7] I'd been wrong to think my life so cheap as to cast it off in a flourish of misguided abandon. I learned it sorely. God's mercy is wide and deep, and no life, even mine, is beyond its reach. His mercy is mightier than every sadness. I knew it now, though only from my sick bed. How I longed to take these lessons so beautifully and torturously won, and bring them to bear in life.

The blessing came at night as I prayed, the flame of the candle my only light. I'd prayed this way many times and had met silence, exhaustion, the lick of a dog in my face, and horses galloping over me. This night, my head thick and ears ringing from pneumonia, there were no tears, no licking dogs, no galloping horses, and in fact, no exhaustion. God knew, as I did, that my mountain had fallen. It seemed that he had withdrawn for a time, to let the pieces fall. I sat on my bed, my candle before me, and asked, "How does one begin again?"

Not by the stuff you're made of, the answer came. *My mercy will cover you like a wind over settling seas.*

How did one pray "thy will, thy will" and mean it? Was God in his heavens? Was life a black comedy? "The pieces would be gathered." I began to write it down. "The empty places shall be filled. Your dignity will guard you. The place I am building is made of precious stones, a foundation of sapphires and gates of carbuncles, not of the ruin of desolate places. Your ache will be your battlements, red as rubies, like blood, powerful and lovely.

"My mercy is as mighty as waters that cannot be held back. The peace of your sons will rush over them like mighty waters. Peace will hound them like the freshness of wind."

How does one explain such things? From where do such words arise?

"My tenderness comes rushing in, water over a desolate land. I myself cannot stay it. My mercy is more powerful than falling mountains. You shall rise in my waters beyond the reach of falling mountains.

"Can you see?"

How does one see?

"Your beginnings have nothing to do with shattered places. I am rebuilding with precious stones. It is your claim on me: My mercy rushes in. I cannot hold it back."

CHAPTER TWELVE

LET GO

My father's multifaceted talents included that of being an artist. Since his death in 1995 my sisters and brother and I have cherished the paintings he left behind. In each of our homes hang visual expressions of his claim on life at its various stages. One sister has "the clown," as we call it, a watercolor depicting a jack-in-the-box type figure before a crowd, his face rendered fluidly with a blurred tragic smile. Then there is my father's "bullfight" and "Pittsburgh bridges." I have a few pastels of a vegetable garden; an oil painting, a train in motion across the Great Plains; and my favorite, the oil in my foyer, dated 1949 — his college days — of a woman in a drooping yellow sun hat and strapless red dress asleep on a New York City apartment balcony. Her head tilts down and her legs are splayed in unselfconscious repose.

I also possess a painting my father did that has been endearingly tagged by family members as *The Floating Boxes* — a departure from his more earthy themes. In describing this painting, I ask the reader to picture a square. Add lines to the four corners of the square, one angled up and right; another down, right; another up and left; the other down, left; all extending to the corners of the painting. This gives the observer the feeling of being inside a box. He painted the four sides of the box in an odd yet astounding combination of colors: lime green, indigo blue, turquoise, pink, tarheel blue. Within that box, my father painted many multicolored smaller boxes of various sizes with the same vivid peculiar coloration: fire orange, muddy brown, olive green, blood red, lemon yellow. The interior boxes float randomly inside the first box, the box that serves as the structure to the painting. Hence the name *Floating Boxes.*

Despite the weird color combinations, the overall effect is lovely and magical in the way my father blended them. Other than that, the painting makes no sense. It did not win a place on anyone's wall. It didn't "fit" into anyone's décor.

When I moved into my home my sister said, "Do you want *The Floating Boxes*? We'll never hang it." I said, "Sure," though I wasn't sure I'd hang it myself. But it was a piece of my father's art, dated 1966, and when I think of my father, the thing I cherish most is his daring creativity. I took the painting, which hangs dead center on the wall in my guest room.

The pneumonia and relapse had debilitated me. The second round of "super" antibiotics killed the infection, but I was yet to spend many more days and weeks in bed with no strength. My body needed to heal. In no small way, I believe, my body's physical collapse was the outward expression of my inner collapse. The whole package needed to heal. There was nothing to do but surrender to my weakness and let my pillows and sheets do their work.

My fever was gone and the doctor had heard no more rattling

sounds coming from my lungs. Still, perhaps brought on by fatigue and the lonely tedium of my illness, I couldn't rally myself to get better. Even in the aftermath of so sublime a movement of God in prayer, there was still a wounding that would mark the final halting steps of this journey.

Agitations had started to overtake me. Still constrained more or less to the confines of my bed, I'd pass the time reading. I'd be moved by great writers. Then I'd roll over to sleep for a while. After a time, agitation about these good books inexplicably gave way to a quiet rage. In healthier days when I'd read a book that moved me, I'd highlight certain parts and later go back and write them in a notebook. During this time, being too tired to write passages in notebooks, I found myself thinking instead: What is one supposed to do with good books? Read, be moved — maybe even profoundly moved — love the authors and dream of meeting them in heaven if they're dead, or on earth if they're not; finish the book; become inspired; put it down; and the very next day forget what it was I'd read that had so moved me? Why go to the trouble to read at all? Was I to keep a notebook of *every book I read* and write down *every moving part*? And what of Chesterton? Was I supposed to rewrite his *entire books* in my notebook? Alone in my bed, my ceiling fan whirring over my head, agitated, immobilized, I'd roll over in the twilight of sleep and wonder why such thoughts afflicted me.

One such book during this time was *A Grief Observed* by C. S. Lewis. I'd read it before, but had gotten little out of it then because life at that stage had not taken its toll. Lewis wrote it in the immediate aftermath of the death of his wife, Joy Davidman. They hadn't been married that long. Before meeting her, he'd been a confirmed, stodgy, and aging bachelor. Late in life they married in an arrangement of convenience, and surprisingly, love found them. Then she died. As Davidman's son Douglas Gresham wrote in the introduction, "for Jack [Lewis] this was the end of so much which life had for so long denied him and then briefly held out to him like a barren promise. For Jack there were none of the hopes . . . of bright sunlight meadows and life-light and laughter."[1]

The tone of the book bears that out. Lewis wrote early on: "Talk to me about the truth of religion and I'll listen gladly. Talk to me about the duty of religion and I'll listen submissively. But don't come talking to me about the consolations of religion or I shall suspect that you don't understand."[2]

Grief is a process, he seemed to say, and even when one resolves to draw boundaries around it, as Lewis did, it returns. Then you find yourself in the dark place you thought you'd just pulled yourself out of. This time 'round, I was understanding what he meant.

In the last chapter Lewis draws a close to his "jottings," as he called them, not because he's passed through the grief but because, he said, if you don't stop yourself at some point, you'll never stop yourself. Sorrow is one of life's few certainties. "It needs not a map but a history," he said, "and if I don't stop writing that history at some quite arbitrary point, there's no reason why I should ever stop."[3]

Lewis raises a daring question about God and the trials he allows his children. "The terrible thing is that a perfectly good God is in this matter hardly less formidable than a Cosmic Sadist," he wrote.

He likens the despair of the Dark Night as the work of the Great Vivisector.

> The more we believe that God hurts only to heal, the less we can believe that there is any use in begging for tenderness. A cruel man might be bribed — might grow tired of his vile sport — might have a temporary fit of mercy.... But suppose that what you are up against is a surgeon whose intentions are wholly good. The kinder and more conscientious he is, the more inexorably he will go on cutting. If he yielded to your entreaties, if he stopped before the operation was complete, all the pain up to that point would have been useless.[4]

"But is it credible," he asks, "that such extremities of torture should be necessary for us?" When people demur and say "I am not afraid of God because I know He is good," Lewis would scoff: "Have they never been to a dentist?"[5]

Children of God are compelled to believe the ordeal of the Dark Night is not vivisection, but wellness, if you survive it. Yet how does one get to the place where he or she perceives the "right Jerusalem blade," as Lewis calls it, as a gift and not as vivisection? Lewis himself, among the greatest of Christian apologists, challenged whether such extremities of torture should be necessary.

Well — *is it?* I wanted to ask Lewis. My agitations intensified and, in a manner of speaking, I confronted the author. "You wrote the book in 1961 and died in 1963. Your torture lasted for only a few years. Then you found your reprieve. What would you say to me now, Mr. Lewis, now that you are on the other side and see those things you only groped for on this side? It is credible?"

I heard Mr. Lewis say, "Hold on."

I said, "What if I can't hold on?"

He said, "Then let go."

That's when I entered the world of the floating boxes.

Into the sixth week of my illness and recovery, my sister had been at my home vacuuming and doing my laundry. She was making motions to leave, coiling cords and putting on her coat. She'd stepped outside to put something in her car when my heart began to race, my chest tightened, and an overpowering feeling of dread took hold of me.

Where am I? I'm sitting on my steps, immobilized and sobbing. I felt the four sides of the box closing in.

My sister came to say good-bye and saw me. She said, "This is bigger than my coming over to help with the laundry."

Where am I? I am walking in circles in my bedroom while my sister pulls clothes from my drawers. She is packing my underwear and grabbing my pillows. She is gathering my things and putting them into a laundry basket.

I slept the rest of that afternoon on the wicker couch on her back porch. Hummingbirds darted about me. Their dog Lucy lay at my feet.

In 1966, when my father painted *The Floating Boxes*, he'd been recovering from a schizophrenic episode in the psychiatric ward of the Cleveland Clinic. He had left us for several months when I was ten, and at the time I never fully understood why. It wasn't until I'd read my grandmother's journals that I became aware of the extent of his illness at that time. Even then, I didn't appreciate the demons he'd fought until the day I sat on my steps unable to help myself. I never reached the levels my dear poor father did. By God's grace he overcame them and lived a complete life. But I came to understand why he painted *The Floating Boxes*. Sitting as I was, helpless and terror-filled, I felt like all the pieces were there, somewhere, but that they floated chaotically, trapped in finite space and unable to fit or become a cohesive whole.

I had "let go," as I'd perceived Lewis saying I should. This is where the journey, in its last flourishes, fell to the ministrations of other good people to see me through to the end.

A novice, when she makes her final vows to become a nun, stands at the altar before the community of sisters and reads her vows. She places her vow paper on the altar and the prioress signs and seals it. The two then stand together while the new sister sings, in alternation with the gathered sisters: "Uphold me, O God, and I shall live and do not fail me in my hope." It is a public affirmation of her dependency upon the community. Her vows, the signature of the prioress, the song come together in the larger confession, "I am not an entity unto myself."[6]

I couldn't hold on, but felt safe enough in letting go. I was not an entity unto myself. And the promise of God proved sound. My sister got me to my doctor. My doctor patched me back together. My son Nate came to stay with me for a few days. And after a week I was functioning again. I could rise in the morning and make my bed. I could fold laundry and get bills in the mail on time. I wrote in my journal a few weeks later, "How far I've come to reach a place where I could lie in bed and read a book in peace. How far I've come to reach level ground. That's all. Nothing more than that."

We don't always see the gifts we're given. The best ones come back again and again, long after the wrapping has been torn away. Lewis said at the end of the book, "Praise in due order; of Him as the giver, of . . . the gift."[7] Praise, even (especially) amid pain, lends it meaning, which gives God meaning and your life meaning. Lewis concludes that *that*, dear one, is "better than nothing."[8]

So the Dark Night is a gift, like loving God: "I must stretch out the arms and hands of love — its eyes cannot here be used," he says. Stretch out your arms in gratitude for the gift, for what it is — not for what you concocted it to be. It is a blade, a tempering tool, a mystery. "Not my idea of God, but God," he says.[9]

I came to understand that if I draw in my mind an image of God in the manner I'd prefer him to assume, and then if I build my story around that idea, or try to, he'll knock it down. Don't think he won't. I am not the architect. Neither are you.

Good Father, earthly parents do not give their children stones.

There have been moments on this journey when I have wondered, *Who would choose, of his or her own reckoning, to take that hand and go down this road?* Frederick Buechner, in his book *Godric,* says, "A man dies many times before he's dead, so does he wend from birth to birth until by grace, he comes alive at last."[10] How many deaths must one die to live? The answer hounded me all the way through to the end: This is the path, the only way to life. When you truly die this death, you give up all questions, and answers too, that incline you to think about where it all might lead. It's the taking of the hand that's the thing. If taking that hand is one's final act on earth, it is sufficient. Even if I am harvested by aliens, what is that to me? I have that hand.

Deep longings in a manner still afflict me. But it has been enough to come to the place of rest where I understand, "You know what I long for, Lord; you hear my every sigh."[11] I went to the bottom and found a place to put my feet. A hand reached for me and I took it. I knew even if I didn't get the answers I craved, I've got that hand. Having it, I knew there was a place I was going and that he was the One taking me there. I hear the words of Augustine: "Now, at last, tired of being misled, entrust to the Truth all that the Truth has given to you and nothing will be lost. All that is withered in you will be made to thrive again. All your sickness will be healed. Your mortal body will be refashioned and renewed and firmly bound to, and when it dies it will not drag you with it to the grave."[12]

Fall

CHAPTER THIRTEEN

MOVE STONES

~~~

*M*y journey through the Dark Night made its final steps in the back roads of Umbria, Italy. My sister and I had planned this trip for months. As it approached, however, the pneumonia and associated weakness had caused me to question whether I could take the trip. My doctor saw me a few days before my departure. She said I was ready. I didn't feel ready. But I trusted her judgment more than my own.

Umbria is a landlocked region in central Italy. Rolling mountains surround an alluvial plain dotted with cypress and elms, mulberries, olive groves, and vineyards. Umbria, no less sublime than its neighboring Tuscany — Italy's "paradigm for heaven" — is marked by limestone crags and hills on lower ridges of the Apennines, dense with pine forests and overlooking valleys of Scotch broom, oxeye daisies, and purple irises. The region boasts the deepest cave system in Italy, with twenty-five miles of underground hideaways that reach 3,000 feet deep.

Tracing the final steps of this journey, even over the back roads of this enchanting locale, I found myself dull of mind and spirit. I remained lethargic, physically weak, laboring, and unaffected.

On the third day, our group ascended a rugged grassy hillside to an isolated medieval fortress known as *Le Due Torri*, the two towers. On this summit an eleventh-century farmhouse and a small chapel rested in the shadows of two watchtowers. In the Middle Ages these would have defended the region against marauders. It was also a stopping place along "the pilgrim's road," which cut through Umbria, north to south, the route traveled on foot by pilgrims from all over Europe, including, tradition says, Peter and Paul. The notion of "pilgrimage" was especially robust during the Middle Ages. Lowly sojourners in brown capes, leather sandals, and black hats set out on foot in pursuit of the "Holy destinations": Rome, Jerusalem, and Santiage de Composteria in Spain. It was not an easy time to be alive in central Italy, given the violence and instability of the age. Times were more daunting for pilgrims who'd plod rugged paths over jutting ridges in bracing winds, seasonal rains, and sometimes even snow, warring factions at their heels. *Le Due Torri* was directly in the path of the primary pilgrimage road through Umbria in the eleventh, twelfth, and thirteenth centuries. It was a resting spot for pilgrims. "Imagine you are pilgrims," our host had said. For the first time on that trip I began to sense there was a reason I'd come. I was a pilgrim, and sensed there was something I ought to be looking for.

Before we left the *Le Due Torri*, our host took me to the small chapel set off from the towers. It was made of whitewashed limestone and stood little more than twelve feet square with a half dozen pews and a small central altar. "Would St. Francis have visited here?" I asked. He explained in humble English that he did not know whether St. Francis had been here. He looked at me earnestly. "Of course everyone knows he was a pilgrim. He walked everywhere. It is probable he stopped here. This location is on the way to many places. We have no records. But we believe he was probably here."

At this moment I felt my journey curiously linked to Francis of Assisi, I can't explain why.

Having made it through what I believed to be the most perilous aspects of this journey, one question still haunted me on this trip: How does one go on living the rest of life with such wounds? The Nicaraguan women had given me the sense of heroic possibility. The pneumonia had imbued me with the sacredness of life itself, on its own terms. My foray into the "floating boxes," brief though it was, enabled me to understand that even when we can't hang on, others will be there to break the fall. Now, in Italy, I was hounded by a question about how to translate these noble aspirations into the wreckage of my life.

St. Francis (whom hereafter I will refer to as Francis) called himself a "churl" and the most vile of sinners, no saint. The legacy of Francis, as I came to understand it during this unexpected pilgrimage, did not arise from his well-known love for animals and nature. It did not arise from the unassailable selfless acts he and the "Little Brothers" (as his band was called) performed among the poorest of the poor. Nor did it arise from the public renunciation of his father's wealth and connections, followed by vows of poverty, chastity, and obedience. Nor did it arise from his well-known fondness for the beautiful Clare, who followed him in a life of renunciation and was numbered among his earliest followers (the first member of the female Second Order, known as the Poor Clares). His legacy, as I owned it, did not arise from the powerful and odd physical manifestation of the wounds of Christ in Francis's own flesh, the stigmata, said to have occurred during a Lenten fast on a mountain precipice near the end of his life.

Francis's legacy came to me in a cave, because he loved caves.

He had been a happy youth, born in 1182 in the medieval fortressed city-state of Assisi, sprawled along the southern slope of Mount Subasio. He was the son of a wealthy cloth merchant, Peter Bernadone, and his wife Pica. His father had been away on business in France at the time of his birth. His mother named him Giovanni, after John the Baptist. Upon his father's return he renamed the child Francesco — "the French one" — a name that carried a father's dreams.

Francis was a little short, with large, kind eyes, bearded, and had delicate hands and a frail physical constitution. He was known to sing songs of the troubadours — French poets who traveled the countryside making melodies of love's sweet longings. He apprenticed his father in the cloth business, happily assuming the role of model and trendsetter for silks and velvets of extravagant colors. His friends, when they'd been drinking, which was often, called him "our *dominus*" — our king. The appellation endeared Francis, and he would sing for them in French and buy another round of drinks. More than once, the name of the young son of Bernadone passed through lips of gossips and barkeeps. He was the leader of a "wild pack of Assisi youths," as one historian puts it, who adds, "This was a sexually anarchic era, and the town was full of randy, undisciplined and hedonistic youngsters. [I]t would be difficult to think of him as diverging from his comrades in only this one area of adolescent experimentation."[1] Even so, Francis was well liked. His extravagant generosity and courtesy extended to all, including the poor.

Assisi went to war with the neighboring city-state of Perugia when Francis was twenty. Bold and heroic as the Assisians were, Francis among them, they were badly outflanked and more or less slaughtered on the field between the two cities. No doubt many of Francis's friends numbered among the dead. He himself was taken prisoner in Perugia where he languished for a year underground with little food, bad water, cold conditions, and no latrine. There he contracted malaria, which would plague him the rest of his days, and probably also the bone tuberculosis pathologists recently determined afflicted him. His father negotiated a ransom for his release. Francis remained bedridden for a year in recovery. He was never the same.

After his recovery he tried in vain to recapture the bliss of profligate youth. But his heart was not in it. He wrestled with depression. In a grand but futile attempt to attain the noble aspiration of knighthood, he joined the papal forces of Walter of Brienne on a Crusade. Barely twenty miles south of Assisi, however, his malarial fever disabled him. He returned home depressed, weakened by illness, and shamed by the sorrow of hopeless dreams.

At the age of twenty-three, while on an errand for his father, he passed a rundown church called San Damiano a mile south of Assisi. He stopped to rest inside the crumbling walls. Francis reposed beneath a Syrian cross hanging over the altar bearing the image of the crucified Christ. He perceived the image was speaking to him. "Francis," it said, "don't you see that my house is being destroyed? Go, then, and rebuild it."

I saw myself a pilgrim. It gave me eyes to look for the unexpected and to imagine possibilities I might not otherwise have been inclined to see.

The latter portion of the trip we stayed in a quaint medieval hill town called Torgiano, a few miles outside of Assisi. The first night I opened the wooden shutters of our room. A church bell rang and birds chattered in the breeze. Then the sky began to change from dullish pink to purple to indigo, then to a dazzling brilliant orange the likes of which neither I nor my sister had ever seen. The sunset seemed to say, *wait and watch*.

The following day we hiked the upper ridge of Mount Subasio, where Francis had walked many times. Hidden within its beech forests and down winding rocky pathways, we took our lunch at a hermitage where Francis often retreated for solitude. I went into a chapel to pray, the only one there not bedecked in a nun's habit of black and white. Bending my aching legs to the hardwood kneeler, I knew I'd never be a nun. I was a hiker, in pain at the moment, my backpack near me on the pew, my boots scraping, shirt smelling, my walking stick within reach. I caught the breeze from an opened window and heard myself pray, "I am a middle-class housewife — I mean, *ex*-housewife." I could see the sun play over the valley. "My knees ache and my eyes hurt," I said. "What does someone like me have to do with that man, Francis?"

The nuns didn't begrudge me my weeping. In a way, I wanted to laugh. I couldn't help thinking I'd taken on a life of poverty, chastity, and obedience without ever joining the Poor Clares!

The kneeler punished my knees. I needed help from my stick to rise. I moved through the hermitage, following steps Francis would have walked, under a narrow stone archway to the lower reaches of a cave. He'd spent many long hours in prayer here. I sat on the rock where he sat and wanted to ask, dear Francis, how many times did your heart break? How does one live out one's life with wounds?

His suffering disabused him of knightly dreams. He renounced the pampered life and acknowledged utter dependence on God. He lived in poverty of hearth and spirit, entrusting himself to an uncharted course, the place where God meets pilgrims. He used to pray with his arms stretched wide, a self-effacing kind of praying. He preached on God's humility, that he so loved his creation, he embraced time and matter. This, for Francis, bestowed holy magnificence to everything on earth and to his existence as well, and most especially to his suffering.

"Who are You, my dearest God? And what am I but Your useless servant?"[2] he prayed often. The last six years of his short life were marked by turmoil, illness, and feelings of failure. He had traveled to Egypt to convert the sultan al-Malik al-Kamil, but failed (though he won his friendship). His eyesight was fading; he couldn't bear to be in daylight. His brotherhood was in crisis, thinking Francis's claim on the gospel too unreasonable. At one point he feared his own order would expel him. "Maybe I should rejoice if they throw me out in shame," he said, "perhaps it would profit my soul."[3] He stepped down as leader and guide. "From now on I am dead to you. But here you have Brother Peter Catanio: let us all, you and I, obey him."[4]

A woman entered the cave where I pondered these things. She wore black and white checked polyester pants and stood near where I sat, my walking stick cradled over a knee. Together in silence, both faces wet, she in polyester and I with my stick, we pilgrims lingered together in that cave seeking strange consolations. Then she left. I turned my face and chafed my cheek against the rock. I'd heard of miracles associated with Francis: the taming of a vicious wolf, preaching to birds who sat and listened. I was a pilgrim. I needed a miracle. So I prayed: "God, I can't go the rest of this journey. Please give me a miracle."

Our last morning in Assisi I made my way alone in the early light, down to the little church of San Damiano, the one Francis rebuilt in accordance with the vision. Here he'd established the Poor Clares, his Little Brothers being located nearby at another church he'd rebuilt. It was to San Damiano (and Clare) Francis retreated near the end of his life when illness and blindness had nearly incapacitated him. He lay day and night in a hut tended to by Clare, unable to endure sun or fire light.

San Damiano, a mile south of Assisi's walls, is tucked down a slope near olive trees with knobby trunks and twisted limbs in tortured reaches for the sun. Mist fell over the valley. A fellow nun in hard shoes with clicking heels made her way down the same road. Behind us clouds hung low over Mount Subasio. Nearing the little church, I passed a stone with words carved into its face: *Il Signore Te Dia Pace,* "the Lord give you peace," Francis's well-known greeting.

I found a spot under a tree behind the church near a cistern. Birds about me, morning's light glinting off the olive trees wet from dew, I thought of Clare, whom Francis had brought here. Some say they'd loved each other, but had renounced it. The life of Francis is a love story in any case. I thought of the question I'd put to dear Francis in my imagination as I sat in the cave that day. How does one finish a life with wounds?

What kind of miracle was I looking for? Did I believe a man could take on the marks of Christ? What do the cries of a middle-class ex-housewife, face to a stone in a cave, have to do with one like him? An ant crawled on me and I hesitated to smash it. I lifted it slowly and placed it in the grass. I heard nuns singing from inside the walls, the same walls Francis built when the voice said "rebuild my church." He had been given a task. He accepted a humble responsibility. From that church where I now sat, the image of the crucified One brought him purpose and rescued him. So he picked up a stone.

He was a pilgrim, stripped of life's easy consolations. Life as a pilgrim had but a single purpose: to have eyes to look for the unexpected, to imagine possibilities, and to remain accessible to the voice that speaks. He heard it and picked up another stone. When he could find none, he begged for stones. Stone upon stone, amid olive groves and singing birds, cooled by morning mists, he moved and piled and scraped until the stones became a wall. The wall became a church. The church became an assertion.

Near the end, as he retreated to this place where I sat, his blindness robbed him of the sun's light and warmth and the beauty of field grass and flowers. With hands that bore scars of nail wounds he composed a song: "No man is worthy to breathe your name. Be praised, my Lord, by all your creatures. In the first place by the blessed Brother Sun who gives us the day and enlightens us through you. He is beautiful and radiant with his great splendor, giving witness of you, most Omnipotent One. Be praised, my Lord by our sister, Mother Earth, who nourishes and watches us while bringing forth abundant fruits with colored flowers and herbs."[5]

He would soon undergo a brutal treatment for his eyes, cauterizing from temple to ear with a red-hot iron and no anesthesia. The fire stoked and the tool lifted, Francis said, "Brother Fire, God has made you beautiful, and strong, and useful. Be courteous with me."

I sat near the spot where the troubadour wrote a song to his love. Why would God have allowed his dear saint to suffer as he did, in a life so freely, happily relinquished? What kind of God is that? Is there beauty in dispossessing what you cannot keep?

At the end of Francis's life, age forty-four, his liver and spleen were distended with lesions. Malarial parasites made him vomit. He found it hard to breathe. The paradox was, even in suffering, his death became an assertion. God acted always only in love. Francis requested of his brothers, as his final gesture on this earth, "When you see that I have come to the end, put me out naked on the ground and allow me to lie there for as long as it takes to walk a leisurely mile."

They lay him naked, face down, and he embraced God's beauty in the dirt. He remembered his dependence on God alone. He whispered to a brother, "I have done what is mine to do. May Christ teach you what is yours to do."

How many times did his heart break? So many, and with such beatitude, the suffering had nowhere to go but to his flesh in the wounds of Christ. How does one live out a life with wounds? I'd asked my question. My answers came through the legacy of Francis. He was disabused of knightly dreams. He acknowledged utter dependence on God, entrusting himself to an uncharted course. He prayed with his arms stretched wide. He so loved God's creation it rendered a holy magnificence to everything on earth, including his own wretched life and especially his suffering. He was a pilgrim, stripped of easy consolations. He had eyes to look for the unexpected, to imagine possibilities, and to remain accessible to the Voice that spoke. He picked up stones. He sang in olive groves in the company of birds, cooled by mists, moving stone upon stone. His humble life became a daring assertion about what God can do with lives that are lost or ill or desperate or without hope.

The miracle wasn't the mental adjustment that allowed me to see that (though it was miracle enough). The miracle was, seeing it, I somehow believed I could appropriate it to my own losses and desperation and hopelessness. I saw in Francis that holy power arises from who we are not; and dependency on God alone covers all we can't do; and if we open ourselves to it (arms wide), surprises await. I didn't see it as giving up or personal surrender of my will and personality. I saw it as a consecration of both, a kind of expansion of the soul. With eyes to see unexpected possibilities, even (especially) in life's wretchedness, and ears to hear the Voice that calls, our hands are freed to pick up stones and render a daring assertion. It is dying with your face to the ground and making even your last breath in the dirt a benediction.

CONCLUSION

BEGINNINGS

Shortly after my return from Italy, I walked around the lake near my home, the Seven Sisters still beautiful even as their colors faded. The bossy white geese still owned their turf, their sassy honkers ordering everybody around. I paid them no mind. I sat on the bench facing the Sisters, near the fountain where a breeze carried water to my face. I saw light refract through fountain mist and understood that life returns like this, in gentle sprays, like water from a fountain in a breeze. Too much life after death would rock you. You might miss a step. Death comes in blows. Life returns in easy sprays.

To this day when I dream at night, I am always on a journey — going somewhere. The nightmares are gone. But the dreams I have don't get me there, wherever it is I'm bound. I'm always on the way. Sometimes I dream I'm still married, or that I'm taking my sons to the dentist. Sometimes I dream someone waits for me behind a closed door, light shining through the crack.

Anyway, as my son said, "You're not dead yet." No, I'm not. I'm alive. And life itself is such a hopeful assertion. Merton calls it "the poetic spirit," — being "content if the flower comes first and the fruit afterwards, in due time."[1]

I was a mother bird with broken wings. I was Maynard taking gruel from a spoon. The earth rocked beneath me but I managed Cassandra just the same. I took what came and what little miracles I could. I found a friend in the desert who lent me his foot, for perspective; he warned me of a gathering storm. I got hit from behind and had my insides pulled out. I landed on the carpet, nose to the Berber, and horses ran over me. It took getting water to the face to remember my baptism. I climbed a mountain and looked upstream, and laid down my fears in a place of death. I took that hand. The aliens came; I didn't cry. Possibility returned at 12:37 AM. I received new clothes, climbing clothes, and God sang a song in the voices of the poor. Sickness made me want to live. Mercies rolled and lifted me beyond debris of falling mountains. Floating boxes frightened me. Others carried me. I went to a cave and asked a question and got my answers in the life of a man who prayed open-armed. Dear Francis helped me move the wreckage of my life, and its questions, not to the place of receiving practical answers but to a landscape where I saw stones to be moved and so I lifted them, one at a time, and have begun to build an assertion. Doing that, Francis taught me how to learn my own name, and the name of Jesus too.

And I believe him.

READER'S GUIDE

CHAPTER ONE: SURRENDER THE TERMS

1. The author mentions the character Franny in J. D. Salinger's book *Franny and Zooey* as having grown weary of "ego, ego, ego." In your opinion, what did Franny mean by that and how does it show itself today?

2. Why would the author have asserted that a divine transaction occurs when the petitioner, in prayer, uses the word "mercy"?

3. In what way did the seekers of John the Baptist discover that their journey had "turned on them"?

4. What does the author mean when she asserts that the good news begins with bad news?

5. Compare and contrast the "Jesus Prayer" (*Jesus, son of David, have mercy on me, a sinner*) and "The Prayer of Jabez" (*Oh, that you would bless me and extend my lands! Please be with me in all that I do, and keep me from all trouble and pain*" [*1 Chronicles 4:10*]) as it has been appropriated in today's context.

6. What "breaches" have you slipped into (if any) wherein you have had to "surrender the terms" of your rescue? What did it feel like?

CHAPTER TWO: BLESS THE MUNDANE

1. What did the author mean when she said, quoting Camus, that "great misfortunes are monotonous"?

2. How did "managing Cassandra" prove helpful?

3. What function does "the mundane" serve in this chapter? What does it suggest about how it should function generally during times of calamity?

4. The Nigerian man read the author the portion from Ephesians that said, "may know . . . the hope of his calling." Why do you think he chose that passage to relate to her? How can one know the hope of God's calling?

5. The pastor at the church she attended said that believing we control our comfort levels is "the antithesis of faith." What did he mean? He also said, "In God's kingdom there is something better than feeling good." What is he referring to?

6. Why do you suppose the author suggested that when she ordered a Michigan cherry pie from Ali's pie-baking business, in a small way, the kingdom of God came down?

Chapter Three: Enter the Chaos

1. The overriding theme in this chapter is the disorientation of chaos. How would you define chaos?

2. The author refers to a dream she had in which a choir director said, "When you sing a masterpiece like this one, even if you don't understand the words, there is something it is trying to say. If you reach that level of perfection, it will say it." What kind of message would a masterpiece be able to communicate that is beyond the understanding of words?

3. The author's son tells her life is "that delicate line between chaos and order." Do you agree with that statement? Is it pos-

sible for "life" to move too far onto one or the other side of that delicate line?

4. Does life seem to you a black comedy or a mystery? (Or nei-ther?)

5. Do you agree with the statements: "Chaos is a way God reveals himself in disparate parts. It helps break him apart into smaller, more manageable pieces"? and that "the ultimate expression of bringing chaos into order is the Cross"? If so, expand your answer. If not, why not?

6. Do you believe the screams and howls of the children on the playground were their singing their parts over and over again, without any notes? And the growls and nervous repetitions in the special needs class were a kind of masterpiece saying what could not be expressed in mere words? Could such utterances indeed be prayers on the edges of chaos? If so, in what way? If not, why not?

CHAPTER FOUR: FOLLOW THE SIGNS

1. Should Christians believe in and act upon "signs"? How can one determine if such a sign has actually come from God?

2. Do you believe we are "hedged around with angelic hosts"? Have you ever experienced a palpable sense of this?

3. What does the author mean when she says meeting the dark-ness opens "oneself to life" and creates a possibility where "the very darkness shines"?

4. How would Cloud Runner "giving his testimony" disarm the demon-owls?

5. When the author suggests that deciding to take a drive that morning was an assertion of hope for a sign, what does this imply about finding "a sign"?

CHAPTER FIVE: NOSE TO THE CARPET

1. The author quotes a Buechner character, Antonio Parr, who said it was the "in-between times, the time narratives like this leave out and that the memory in general loses track of, which are the times when souls are saved or lost." What did Parr mean by that? How did it fit into the scenario the author faced at the time?

2. What does the author suggest when she says, It takes a certain violence to reach the innermost recesses of the Dark Night. "Who would go voluntarily? Losses, wreckages, stabbings, and displacement drive you there, down, down until there is no farther down to go. And there you are."

3. The author said sometimes in prayer the knees didn't seem low enough, so she'd bow. Does physical posture really affect our praying?

4. What do you think the author meant when she wrote, "Worshiping God in the beauty of holiness comes in little things that add up to a big thing, a cosmic thing"?

5. Why do you think she perceived the beauty of holiness in the church in Ecuador when hands started going up to give back communion cups?

CHAPTER SIX: TRAMPLE THE DESPAIR

1. What could the author have meant when she said sometimes reflected light cannot be held by a single sphere?

2. The author describes the feeling of despair as "wearing a blood-stained coat." In your own words, how would you define despair?

3. She cites Thomas Merton who wrote, This, then, is our desert: to live facing despair, but not to consent. "Trample it down under hope in the Cross. Wage war against despair unceasingly." How did the author answer the challenge? How would you answer it?

4. The author includes the words from the sermon she heard the day she decided to return to church: "It is tempting to become like the Hebrews who did not want to leave their homes in Babylon. But that is not the way of the Lord." What do those words mean to you, and in what way do you think they left an impact on the author in her circumstances?

5. The author seemed moved by the ceremonial reenactment of the sprinkling of holy water: "By this water of baptism" . . . and the children echoed: "Remember your baptism." What in your opinion would be the point of this ritual? What would be the benefit of someone remembering his or her baptism?

CHAPTER SEVEN: FACE UPSTREAM

1. What is the point of Annie Dillard's statement about meeting life by facing upstream? Why would she include the rebuke, "Just simply turn around; have you no will?"

2. The author makes reference to the question posed by her pastor in a sermon: "We ask in times of trouble, *Where is God?*" and to the answer given to his own question: "Wherever there is suffering, God is there." How does this thought relate to Jesus' cleansing of the Temple?

3. What does Jesus' indignation tell us about those who are seeking to know God?

4. The author describes her feelings the first time she "went to the rail" to receive the sacrament. She said, "I felt the waters close around me and seaweed wrapping itself around my head." What, in your opinion, prompted her to feel this way?

5. How, if at all, is going to the rail to receive the body and blood of Christ like facing upstream?

6. This chapter highlights the healing power of nature. Do you agree? What experiences in nature have had a healing effect in your life?

CHAPTER EIGHT: STRIP YOUR ALTAR

1. The author quotes Thomas Merton, who called the spiritual death of the Dark Night "the awful dereliction of the soul closed in upon itself." How do you define a soul that has closed in upon itself?

2. In pondering the humiliations Jesus met before his crucifixion, the author concludes, "What else could they do to the One who had laid bare their consciences?" What did she mean?

3. Is it possible for someone who considers him or herself an authentic believer to be living only a "half-life" in the spiritual sense, as the author calls it?

4. Why would Jesus have left "foot washing" as his model for leadership and "ministry"? Have you ever washed anyone's feet or had your feet washed?

5. What is your greatest fear? Have you laid it down in the darkness where Jesus laid down his fear?

CHAPTER NINE: RECEIVE YOUR NEW GARMENTS

1. Describe in your own words the point of the journey when, for the author, she reached the nadir and stepped across the invisible line that began the ascent.

2. A kind of hope returned to her, she said, but not the kind that made her swoon over dreams, nor her head spin over undefined promises of future happiness. What, then, was the nature of her newfound hope?

3. The author quotes Augustine who described the process she experienced as "laboring under the pain of the new life that was taking birth." Have you ever undergone a similar kind of labor?

4. Why do you think the nurse described the comment of the little boy — "When I start to die will it hurt?" — as the most courageous thing she had ever heard?

5. The author likens the service of dedication of the new altar hangings to the moment she felt her bloodstained jacket had been removed and replaced with new garments. What brought her to the place where she could affirm this possibility?

CHAPTER TEN: HOLD ON! HOLD ON!

1. The author quotes the words from a prayer: God is "singing his song in the hearts of the poor." How did these words prove true for her during her trip to Nicaragua?

2. How did Maritza begin to find hope in God, and that he "sends someone to each of us to give us hope . . . the hand that is trying to reach me"?

3. How did the author perceive the people she met as becoming her miracle?

4. What "song" did she hear in these voices? How did they aid her in her ascent?

5. What, if anything, did you take away from this chapter in learning about the poor?

CHAPTER ELEVEN: FIGHT FOR AIR

1. In describing the blessing that came from this journey, along with its wounding, the author quoted Frederick Buechner's *Son of Laughter,* when Jacob wrestled with God: "I remember as blessing the one glimpse I had of his face. It was more terrible than the face of dark, or of pain, or of terror. It was the face of light." What did he mean? Why did the author cite it?

2. She describes how her "ache had defaulted to physical capitula-tion — the emotional turned physiological." Do you believe there is a relationship between the inner state and one's physi-cal well-being?

3. She quotes Albert Camus, who wrote in his novel, *The Plague*, "Our townsfolk . . . forgot to be modest, that was all, and

thought everything still was possible for them; which presupposed that pestilences were impossible." What is he saying? Is it wrong to think "everything is possible"?

4. She describes how she began to "pray the hours" to tap into the higher rhythm of God, believing in the rhythms of prayer. What was her thinking? Why did she undertake this type of systematic praying? Were her thoughts ill-conceived?

5. She came to understand life itself was God's sacred mysterious gift, and not its "passing identities." Do you agree with this? If so, what is the point of "passing identities" in one's life?

6. She heard in prayer God speak to her saying, "Your beginnings have nothing to do with shattered places. I am rebuilding with precious stones." What does this mean, in your opinion? How did the author find solace in it?

CHAPTER TWELVE: LET GO

1. The author makes the point that as her recovery wore on, even as the pneumonia itself had been overcome, she could not regain her health. What does she speculate is the reason for this? What does it suggest about human nature and community?

2. She also describes how even after so "sublime a movement of God" during a time of prayer, she still slipped and fell in the final halting steps of her journey. What does this suggest about the nature of growth in God? How can we persevere when we fall?

3. The author cites C. S. Lewis, in *A Grief Observed*: "Talk to me about the truth of religion and I'll listen gladly. Talk to me

about the duty of religion and I'll listen submissively. But don't come talking to me about the consolations of religion or I shall suspect that you don't understand." What is he referring to when he says anyone who speaks of the "consolation of religion" does not understand?

4. What does Lewis mean when he says sorrow "needs not a map but a history"? And why does the author cite this passage?

5. How would you answer the question, "Is it credible that such extremities of torture should be necessary?" Elaborate: Necessary for what?

6. In her imaginary conversation with Lewis during which the author asks him that same question and he tells her to "hold on," how is he answering her? Is he saying yes? Or no? What does he imply about his answer when he tells her to "let go"?

7. How did the author come to see the journey of the Dark Night as a gift and not vivisection?

8. What did the author mean when she said, "praise, even (especially) amid pain, lends it meaning, which gives God meaning and your life meaning"?

CHAPTER THIRTEEN: MOVE STONES

1. What are your thoughts about the notion of "pilgrimage" as it was expressed robustly during the Middle Ages? Is there anything to be gained by becoming lowly sojourners in brown capes, leather sandals, and black hats who set out on foot in pursuit of the "Holy destinations"? If so, what? If not, why not?

2. How did the author's sense that she was a pilgrim change her demeanor on her trip? What made the difference?

3. What is the author's thought about the purpose of St. Francis praying with his arms stretched wide? Have you ever prayed that way? Are you willing to?

4. The author came to the cave with a question and prayed for a miracle. What was the answer to her question, and how did she perceive her miracle? Would you call it a miracle?

5. What is the power the author perceived arising from who we are not; and the dependency she said covers what we can't do; and the surprises she said await letting go what we can't keep? Do you agree?

NOTES

INTRODUCTION
1. *St. Francis of Assisi* (New York: Image Doubleday), p. 65.
2. Hebrews 5:7-9, NLT.
3. George Buttrick, *Prayer* (New York: Abingdon, 1942), p. 114.
4. Dante, *The Divine Comedy, Hell,* translated by Dorothy Sayers (New York: Penguin, 1949), p. 119.
5. John 6:68, the rendering.
6. Thomas Merton, *No Man Is an Island* (New York: Harcourt Brace Jovanovich, 1955), p. 81.

CHAPTER ONE
1. Psalm 81:10.
2. Matthew 3:10.
3. Matthew 11:7-9.
4. Matthew 11:12.
5. J. D. Salinger, *Franny and Zooey* (Boston: Little, Brown and Co., 1955), pp. 33-37.

CHAPTER TWO
1. We used contrasting versions: I, the *New Living Translation*; he, the *King James Version*.
2. Psalm 107:29-30.
3. Psalm 122:3,5-6.

CHAPTER THREE
1. Frederick Buechner, *The Eyes of the Heart* (San Francisco: HarperSanFrancisco, 1999), p. 16.
2. George MacDonald, *Phantastes* (Grand Rapids, Mich.: Eerdmans, 2000), pp. 119-120.

3. George Buttrick, *Prayer* (New York: Abingdon, 1942), p. 30.

4. John 6:55-56.

5. John 6:66.

6. John 15:7, the translation.

7. Deuteronomy 31:6, NKJV.

8. Thomas Merton, *Dialogues with Silence,* edited by Jonathan Montaldo (San Francisco: HarperSanFrancisco, 2001), p. 135.

CHAPTER FOUR

1. David Steindl-Rast with Sharon Lebell, *The Music of Silence* (Berkley, Calif.: Seastone, 1998), p. 21.

2. Steindl-Rast and Lebell, p. 21.

CHAPTER FIVE

1. Portions of 1 Chronicles 16:29-35, NKJV.

2. Frederick Buechner, *The Book of Bebb: Open Heart* (Book Two) (San Francisco: HarperSanFrancisco, 2001), p. 181.

CHAPTER SIX

1. Malachi 2:16: "'I hate divorce,' says the LORD, the God of Israel. 'It is as cruel as putting on a bloodstained coat.'"

2. Thomas Merton, *No Man Is an Island,* (New York: Harcourt Brace Jovanovich, 1955), p. 236.

3. Merton, *No Man Is an Island,* p. 228.

4. Thomas Merton, *Thoughts in Solitude* (New York: Farrar, Straux, Giroux, 1956), pp. 5-8.

5. *The Book of Common Prayer* (New York: Oxford University Press, 1990), p. 308.

6. *The Book of Common Prayer*, pp. 306-307.

CHAPTER SEVEN

1. Annie Dillard, *Pilgrim at Tinker Creek* (New York: Harper Perennial, 1974), p. 101.

2. Dillard, p. 118.
3. Dillard, p. 3.
4. Jonah 2:1-9, taken from the version read during the worship
   service as it is found in the liturgy.
5. Dillard, pp. 38, 62, 118, 129, 176, 229, 239, 242.
6. Dillard, p. 270.
7. Psalm 46:3,5.

CHAPTER EIGHT
1. Thomas Merton, *Contemplative Prayer* (New York: Image, 1971),
   p. 109.
2. Psalm 22, read at the service.
3. Taken from Psalms 3:8 and 18:5,9,11.

CHAPTER NINE
1. Augustine, *Confessions* (New York: Penguin, 1961), p. 168.
2. Adapted from *The Book of Common Prayer* (New York: Oxford
   University Press, 1990), p. 815.
3. Psalm 30:11.

CHAPTER ELEVEN
1. Frederick Buechner, *Son of Laughter* (San Francisco:
   HarperSanFrancisco, 1993), pp. 161-162.
2. John Donne, *The Complete Poetry & Selected Prose of John Donne,* edited
   by Charles M. Coffin (New York: The Modern Library, 1994),
   p. 415.
3. Albert Camus, *The Plague* (New York: Vintage, 1991), p. 35.
4. *The Book of Common Prayer* (New York: Oxford University Press,
   1990), p. 460.
5. Adapted from *The Book of Common Prayer*, p. 461.
6. Adapted from *The Book of Common Prayer*, p. 133.
7. Camus, p. 164.

CHAPTER TWELVE

1. C. S. Lewis, *A Grief Observed* (San Francisco: HarperSanFrancisco, 1961), p. xxv.
2. Lewis, p. 25.
3. Lewis, pp. 59-60.
4. Lewis, p. 43.
5. Lewis, p. 43.
6. Joan Chittister OSB, *Wisdom Distilled from the Daily* (San Francisco: HarperSanFrancisco, 1990), p. 134.
7. Lewis, p. 62.
8. Lewis, p. 63.
9. Lewis, p. 67.
10. Frederick Buechner, *Godric* (San Francisco: HarperSanFrancisco, 1980), p. 99.
11. Psalm 38:9.
12. Augustine, *Confessions* (New York: Penguin, 1961), p. 81.

CHAPTER THIRTEEN

1. Donald Spoto, *Reluctant Saint* (New York: Viking Compass, 2002), p. 28.
2. Spoto, p. 170.
3. Spoto, p. 185.
4. Spoto, p. 173.
5. Julien Green, *God's Fool*, translated by Peter Heinegg (San Francisco: Harper & Row, 1985), pp. 256-257; I have changed his choice of word "through" for the English word "by" in keeping with the version as it appears in *The Little Flowers of St. Francis*, translated by P. Leone Bracaloni (Assisi: Edizioni Porziuncula, 1982).

CONCLUSION: BEGINNINGS

1. Thomas Merton, *Raids on the Unspeakable* (New York: New Directions, 1964), pp. 159-160.

ABOUT THE AUTHOR

Wendy Murray Zoba is an award-winning writer and author of nine books, including *Sacred Journeys* and *Generation 2K*.

She earned a bachelor of arts degree from Hiram College, Hiram, Ohio, and completed a master's degree in theological studies in New Testament at Gordon-Conwell Theological Seminary. She lived in Honduras for four years where she served as regional reporter for *Time* magazine.

Upon her return to the United States she worked at *Christianity Today* magazine as an associate editor and senior writer, and presently serves as editor of GOD magazine. She has also written for *Books & Culture*, *The Christian Century*, and *Beliefnet.com*. Twice, her essays have been included in *The Best Christian Writing* (2002 and 2004).

Wendy has three grown sons and lives in western North Carolina.